REFLECTIONS FROM THE INNER LIGHT

Reflections *from* *the* Inner Light

A Journal of Quaker Spirituality

JAMES R. NEWBY

RESOURCE *Publications* · Eugene, Oregon

REFLECTIONS FROM THE INNER LIGHT
A Journal of Quaker Spirituality

Resource Publications
An Imprint of Wipf and Stock Publishers
199 W. 8th Ave., Suite 3
Eugene, OR 97401

www.wipfandstock.com

PAPERBACK ISBN: 978-1-5326-8617-7
HARDCOVER ISBN: 978-1-5326-8618-4
EBOOK ISBN: 978-1-5326-8619-1

Manufactured in the U.S.A.   JULY 2, 2019

To Darlene and John . . .
Without whom I would not have been
the infamous middle child

Out in front of us is the drama of persons and of nations, seething, struggling, laboring, dying. Upon this tragic drama in these days our eyes are all set in anxious watchfulness and in prayer. But within the silences of the souls of persons an eternal drama is ever being enacted, in these days as well as in others. And on the outcome of this inner drama rests, ultimately, the outer pageant of history.

—THOMAS KELLY, *A TESTAMENT OF DEVOTION*

Contents

Acknowledgments

"WRITING IS THE PROCESS one follows to learn what is already known deep within," wrote Mary Anne Radmacher. And for me, such a creative process of learning is always a corporate experience as well as one of individual solitude. I am grateful to many who have helped to inspire this work. To my wife, Elizabeth, for her love, encouragement and support. To my daughter, Alicia Marie and her husband, David, who have been loving encouragers. To my friends in Oriental, North Carolina, but especially to my dear friend, Captain Larry Walker, who provided the diversion necessary for a healthy and balanced life during most of the time I was writing. Larry has passed from this world since I began this work, but I have felt his presence in every word I have written. To my beloved community of faith, Cincinnati Friends Meeting, who first heard many of these thoughts in classes or when I spoke out of the silence on First Day morning, and to Debbie Overmyer, willing editor and friend. To my spiritual mentors, Elton Trueblood, Scotty Peck, Jim Kavanaugh, Howard Thurman, Frederick Buechner, Anne Lamott, Sam Keen, John Woolman, Julian of Norwich, etc. And some of my current day Quaker colleagues, Parker Palmer, Phil Gulley and Brent Bill. Many I have known in the flesh, and others I know only through their writings. For their gifts of modeling authenticity, trust and love, I am grateful.

Finally, I thank my older sister, Darlene, and my younger brother, John. Though our life paths and geography separate us, we share the common experience of being the children of Richard and Doris. It was with you that I began my spiritual journey, my process of discerning guidance from the Light Within, and it is to you that I dedicate this work.

Introduction

Trying to Sort It All Out

"I AM JUST TRYING to sort it all out." He looked tired and strained as he held his head in his hands, weeping. John had been diagnosed with an inoperable brain tumor, and I was meeting with him just a day after he and his family had received the news. John called it a "death sentence," and now he was thinking about life issues that before this tragic news he had thought about with only passing attention. *Why me? Why did God do this to me? How will my family survive without me? How do I live the rest of my life? What is God really like?* Such questions were all a part of our conversation, and there would be many more questions in the days to come. "I'm just trying to sort it all out." Although John's "sorting" process was now on a fast track because of his diagnosis, we are all involved in such a process, a process that takes a lifetime to work through. Each one of us is at different places along this *sorting continuum*, but regardless of stage of life, education or profession, we are all on it.

This volume is my written testimony to the ways that I, a white male from North America, reared in the Quaker tradition, have been seeking to understand this life and my purpose in it. Quakers would call this *discernment*. I have tried to imagine what my life would have been like with different parents, a different neighborhood, a different faith tradition. How did it happen that I was born a white male in Midwest America? Why not black or Hispanic? Why not Mississippi instead of Minnesota? And why not sharecroppers for parents instead of a Quaker minister and a musician? I don't know. I do know that the family in which I was reared and the culture in which I was formed has made me who I am. As Quaker author Philip Gulley reminds us, "Our first community is never one we choose. It is chosen for us, usually by our parents and the accidents of biology. It consists of parents, siblings, grandparents, aunts, uncles, and cousins." Of course, there have been choices, the person I would marry, the college I would attend, and so on. My choices, however, have been played out mostly within the confines of family tradition and cultural influences.

In the movie, *Forrest Gump*, Forrest stands over the grave of his wife, Jenny, talking to her. His monologue has to do with whether our lives are planned, and whether each of us has a destiny to fulfill, or if we just float through life like a feather in the wind, going wherever the wind takes us. Forrest concludes, as I would conclude, "I think it is both."

Life presents us with many and varied experiences, all of which offer us opportunities for spiritual growth. Some have experienced such growth through the traditions and practices within their faith communities, or, like St. Francis or the Quaker, John Woolman, in times of connecting with the natural world. A deepening connection with God can come through reading the Bible, the classics of devotion, a novel, or through a simple conversation with a friend. Such growth also comes, as it did for John, in the sad realization that one's physical life is in peril. Such news focuses our minds and our hearts on the most important task in our lives, *spiritual growth,* which is the hoped-for outcome of seeking to connect with what Quakers call, the Inner Light.

In the pages that follow, I present the primary ways in which I have grown spiritually. As I have edited this work for publication, I noticed that two words appear quite often, *experience* and *process.* All authors have pet words and phrases that tend to show up more than once in a work, and I thought about how I might change the use of these two words to be less repetitive. The more I thought about a change, however, the more I realized that the words *experience,* and *process* define what *journaling* is all about.

We experience, and we process. This is the discipline of reflective thought.

I have divided the chapters in this *journal* into five parts, representing the main areas of my spiritual growth: *Turning Inward, Community and Relationship, Pain and Growth, Path of a Seeker,* and *Affirmations.* Each chapter concludes with queries to encourage readers to reflect upon their own spiritual journeys. Readers may find some of what I write humorous, or some passages may provoke tears. Still others may challenge and prompt readers to question their beliefs. Humor and tears, spiritual challenges and questions, are all of God, for to grow in spirit encompasses all the feelings and emotions through which we pass in this life. Unlike John, my process is not yet on a fast track. I do, however, process my life with the ever-increasing knowledge that my physical existence is terminal. In the words of my late friend and author Malcolm Muggeridge, "Every happening great and small is a parable whereby God speaks to us, and the art of life is to get the message." These *reflections* are my attempt to get the message.

JAMES R. (JIM) NEWBY
Newbeginnings
Oriental, North Carolina

Part I.

TURNING INWARD

1.

Silence and the Inner Light

. . . an intensified pause, a vitalized hush,
a creative quiet . . .

SILENCE HAS ALWAYS PLAYED the central role in my spiritual development. As the son of a Quaker minister, each First Day, (Sunday to the world beyond Quakers), would begin by "going to meeting." As we would find our regular seats in the little Friends Meetinghouse in Minneapolis, Minnesota (my home community for the first eight years of my life) my mother would turn to me and my siblings, raise her finger to her lips and politely "shhhhhh-hhhhhh" us. This was followed by the familiar words which every Quaker knows by heart, "It is time to center down and mind the Light." I knew the routine, and early in life I learned that in this experience of quiet seeking the Sacred and the human could meet. It was hallowed ground.

My family can trace its Quaker roots to the mid-seventeenth century when George Fox, the founder of Quakerism, began his ministry in northern England. The Newby name is found in several accounts of early Friends' work. One of my relatives paid a particularly high price for her faith. In his book, *The Beginnings of Quakerism, Vol. 1*, William Braithwaite shares the story of

Margaret Newby, a distant cousin, who dared to share her faith in public in 1655, thirty-four years before the Act of Toleration of 1689. Braithwaite explains: "The place had already earned the name of 'the persecuting town of Evesham' when in the middle of a cold November two women Friends in Westmoreland, Margaret Newby and Elizabeth Cowart, came to it. After a large meeting, they went to visit prisoners. The townspeople were excited against the Quakers, and when one of the women, Margaret Newby, began to address them she was arrested and put in the stocks." Margaret Newby was left in the stocks and in the cold damp weather for seventeen hours. As a result of this exposure, she later died. Her life and her witness were a source of enduring hope and strength for many others.

The Newbys eventually migrated to America, settling on the coast of North Carolina in Perquimans and Pasquotank counties. Here they joined several Friends who had migrated earlier, and helped establish the Piney Woods Meeting, now the oldest continuous place of worship in North Carolina.

The most important contribution that Quakers have made to the world of theology is the belief that every person has within himself or herself an Inner Light of God, and that silence is the best way to connect with this Light. "Silence is a natural demand born of a need for God, felt by young and old, in all the world's religions," begins a statement adopted by the Friends General Conference. It continues, "In silence we may worship together, sharing our search for life, sharing our quest for peace, sharing God's gift of love." While recognizing that silence is just the medium used to connect with the Inner Light, silence can sometimes be a dead form or an occasion to sleep. However, and this is what my mother's shhhhhhhhhhhh was about, it may be, to quote Rufus Jones, a Friend of an earlier generation, "an intensified pause, a vitalized hush, a creative quiet, an actual moment of mutual and reciprocal correspondence with God."

Wow! "An actual moment of mutual and reciprocal correspondence with God." In other words, in silence, God, the Creator of the Universe, could meet with me, a small boy in Minnesota, and impart whatever Godly wisdom he or she wished to impart. The idea of such an encounter was "heady" and "heart" stuff for a seven-year-old, and I took this possibility very seriously. With eyes closed so tightly they hurt, and hands clasped so firmly I nearly cut-off the blood supply, I waited, and waited.

"Spiritual examination is the goal of Quaker silence," J. Brent Bill has written in his book, *Holy Silence.* "At its most basic, it can be as simple as using the silence as a time of asking questions about ourselves. Do I see my time, talents, energy and money as gifts from God? Do I buy more stuff because I need it, or to impress my neighbors or myself?"

Silence, a time for slumber or a time to connect with the Inner Light of God and spiritually examine our lives. In our day of loud traffic and music, of yelling politicians and evangelists, silence is a rare commodity. But silence, I am convinced, is the place where spiritual growth begins. To quiet the competing voices within, and the clamor without, is to provide that time and space necessary to hear the "still small voice" of the Living God.

In the busyness of life that entraps us, may we try to find that silent chamber where we can be still and examine ourselves spiritually. May we open our hearts and minds to the Inner Light of God. Each time that we are distracted from the stillness, let us quietly return to holy silence.

What are your first memories of quiet solitude wherein
you encountered the transforming possibilities of silence?

Do you find regular intervals throughout your day when
you can be still and seek to connect with
the Inner Light of God?

2.

Where Words Come From

I love to feel where words come from . . .

HIS NAME WAS PAPUNEHANG. Although I have always had
difficulty pronouncing and spelling his name correctly, his words
spoken over two hundred years ago have had a lasting effect on
my spiritual life. As the story goes, the eighteenth century Quaker,
John Woolman, best known for his efforts to abolish slavery, and of
whom I write extensively in chapter 25, felt "led of God" to travel
among the American Indians in western Pennsylvania. On that
incredible journey, Woolman's physical life was in constant dan-
ger. Upon arrival in a certain Native American village, Woolman
invited some of the inhabitants, Chief Papunehang among them,
to sit in silence and worship with him. At the close of this time
that Quakers would call, "Silent waiting upon God," Papunehang
turned to Woolman, and through an interpreter said, "I love to feel
where words come from."

The story is a classic in Quaker circles. The spoken words of
Chief Papunehang reach into the heart and soul of what meditative
silence can do and mean. Within that feeling, words are expressed,
both inwardly and outwardly, and transformation occurs. As a
form of spiritual expression, words by themselves are imperfect,

and feelings unexpressed repress our souls. But when feeling and word combine, we reach into the souls of one another, and spoken and unspoken words are shared. In such reflective silence, we become spiritually aware, and being spiritually aware, we become self aware and socially aware of our human interconnectedness.

I have been asked on numerous occasions, "How do you define spiritual?" Good question. For me, the word is elusive and is difficult to define fully. This mysterious quality is important, and I believe the word will always elude capture and exact definition. Our human vocabulary needs such words, words that are always just beyond our grasp, in a region where we travel more by faith (another elusive word) than by sight, more by experiential feeling than by logical reason. And so, when I use the word spiritual or spirituality, all those who are travelers and seekers in the mysterious realm of faith will understand what is meant, but not fully. All our experiences in this realm are unique to those experiencing them.

Words can provoke life stories and experiences, where, upon reflection, we can track the guidance of the Inner Light. To *feel* words, rather than defining them intellectually, or merely using them as a form of verbal or written communication, is to begin the process of connecting with that Divine Center that resides within each of us, and out of which we are moved into the realm of transforming spiritual growth. Words are not the experiences, but they can be one means to take us there.

When separated from the Inner Light, words can be hurtful and spiritually destructive. We all know what it is like to be the perpetrator of careless, hurtful language, or to be on the receiving end of a verbal attack. However, there are words when spiritually felt that can take us to that inner sanctuary where Chief Papunehang could feel "where words come from." We can experience spiritual growth through the spirituality of expression: One cannot read *the Beatitudes* and not feel them spiritually. One cannot read Lincoln's *Gettysburg Address* and not be moved spiritually.

An old Chinese proverb says, "Words are the keys to the heart." This sentiment was certainly true for Papunehang. In spiritual silence, words that are "keys to the heart" are formed. And when we have learned through the discipline of silent waiting how to feel where words come from, we can experience how we are being quietly taught the ways of God.

How have words affected you spiritually?

Can you relate to Papunehang in his expression,
"I love to feel where words come from?"

3.

Transforming Moments

I am not the man I was . . .

IN 1981, TWO IMPORTANT books were released. Both sought to explain how one can understand spiritual experiences. One of these volumes was Jim Fowler's *Stages of Faith Development*, and the other was Jim Loder's *The Transforming Moment*. Each book is important in its own way, and I have used both in my teaching.

As much as I respect the work of Jim Fowler and his groundbreaking book, I have found myself more and more captivated by what Loder calls, "transforming moments." Because of Jim Loder and his work on *transformation*, I decided to do my doctoral work at Princeton Theological Seminary, where he taught.

I love transformation stories. I enjoy reading or hearing about the flashes of light from heaven that transformed Saul to Paul along the Damascus road. Or there is the wonderful transformational experience of Ebenezer Scrooge following his confrontation with the Ghosts of Christmas Past, Christmas Present and Christmas Future in Charles Dickens' *A Christmas Carol*. Scrooge exclaims toward the end of this classic, "I am not the man I was!"

History, and specifically Christian history, is filled with stories of such transforming moments. There was St. Augustine who heard voices of children saying, "Take up and read. Take up and read." And when he picked up his little volume of the Apostle Paul's Letters, and read, his eyes fell on a passage in Romans (Romans 13:13-14) which changed his life, and subsequently, Western civilization. There was the moment when George Fox heard a voice that declared, "There is one, even Christ Jesus, who can speak to thy condition." There was the time John Wesley, the father of Methodism, heard Luther's Commentary on Romans being read, and his heart was "strangely warmed." Blaise Pascal had a transforming experience on November 23, 1654, writing, "From about half past ten in the evening until about half past twelve . . . FIRE. God of Abraham, God of Isaac, God of Jacob, not of philosopher's and scholars. Certitude, certitude, feeling, joy and peace . . . Let me never be separated from him." It has been reported that Pascal wrote these words on a piece of paper that he had sewn into his coat so that he could keep them close to his heart.

In a different context, there is the experience of my friend, Tom Tipton, whose biography *Shining Out and Shining In* I wrote a few years ago. Tom is best known as the soloist for Robert Schuller's *Hour of Power* television program. He says, "In April 1968, Dr. Martin Luther King Jr. was murdered in Memphis, and then in June, Senator Robert Kennedy was killed in Los Angeles. I was on the couch resting, watching the returns from the California Democratic primary, and then it happened. Bobby Kennedy was shot. It was around 1:00 in the morning in Washington, DC. I saw the whole thing. And the Holy Spirit came over me. Now I don't know much about the Holy Spirit, but I certainly felt the Spirit that night. I looked up and said, 'Okay Lord, you are speaking to me.' And the Spirit said that I needed to go to Minnesota and serve." This was a pivotal, transforming moment in the life of Tom Tipton.

In my own life I have had such a transforming moment. My dear friend and mentor, Elton Trueblood, had died in December 1994, and my marriage of twenty-five years seemed to be at an end. In an effort to complete two book projects, I was spending the month of February on the coast of North Carolina. The burdens on my heart were overwhelming, and although I was still functional, I felt lonely and depressed. Since the death of my father, life had become a litany of loss. While I was away for this month, my primary motivation to get out of bed in the morning was the anticipation of seeing the sun rise over the beautiful Atlantic Ocean. And so, on this tenth day of my self-imposed exile at the coast, I awakened to the smell of coffee brewing, and dressed in my running suit for my ritual walk to the beach.

The condominium where I was staying was not more than seventy-five yards from the water. The sun was already casting a pink glow across the horizon, and the ocean waves were rhythmically pounding the shore. It was cold that morning, perhaps in the mid-thirties. Everything seemed crisp and alive. I stared off into the vastness of the ocean and began to weep. I lamented where my life on this earth had brought me. Many years worth of repressed pain flowed up from the pit of my stomach, creating a torrent of tears. Hiding my face behind my cup of coffee, I sat down in the sand.

What occurred next is difficult to describe. As clearly as if someone were seated next to me, I heard the words, "Everything is going to be all right." I was startled and began to glance from side to side looking for the source of that reassuring declaration. Again, "Everything is going to be all right." There was no one on the beach but me.

I stood up, took my last gulp of coffee, and began to walk the narrow, sandy path back to my February home. The words, from wherever they had come, brought a strange sense of comfort. "Everything is going to be all right." I was beginning to sense that my personal chaos had been tinged with the Sacred. The words provided a lining of hope in one of my neediest hours. That was a profoundly spiritual experience, an experience that I felt, and can only be understood by those who have known similar experiences. I believe that the Infinite had reached out to me, a finite man on a lonely North Carolina beach, and I have not been the same since.

All these experiences represent moments when the Living God confronted the human condition and as a result, those who lived these experiences moved in an entirely different direction.

Such moments give meaning to the rest of life, and while we are in those moments, and reflect upon them, they define for us who we are, where we are going, and how we are going to get there.

We cannot *think* our way into transformation, nor can we induce such experiences. We can, however, do certain things to cultivate an expectation of such transforming moments, or what I call, *a density of readiness*.

I am helped spiritually in the preparation of such readiness by the classic disciplines of prayer, meditative silence, the reading of Scripture and the classics of devotion. All these disciplines help sensitize my spirit and cultivate my reverence for God. What have been called the *Yokefellow Disciplines* have become my disciplines:

- To pray, everyday, preferably at the beginning of the day.

- To read a portion of Scripture, reverently and thoughtfully every day.

- To share, at least once each week, in the public worship of God, within a beloved community of faith.

- To give a definite portion of my annual income to promote causes that will serve humanity.

- To use my time as a sacred gift not to be wasted, striving to make my daily work a vocation of ministry and caring.

- To try, every day, to lift some human burden.

- To develop my mental powers by careful reading and study.

I am also helped in developing a density of readiness by placing myself face to face with human suffering. My soul is sensitized when I visit a hospital or homeless shelter to encourage those who are feeling hopeless. Such a confrontation with human suffering could mean a mission trip to Belize or Mexico, or a visit to the southern border where some of our fellow human beings are being held in cages. To be in touch with human suffering opens our hearts and our souls to transformation.

I have also found that sharing my story in a confessional way, and allowing others the opportunity to recount their stories, cleanse the windows of spiritual perception. The soul needs friendship that is without pretense and without the need to play the game of social respectability. In such friendships there is no fear of expressing deep emotion.

When I take time to savor the beauty of God's creation my soul is sensitized. Walks in gardens and drives through the country are meaningful ways to develop a density of readiness. Lingering meditation at the sight of a sunrise or sunset are also ways our souls become open to transformational possibilities.

Each of us will experience God in different ways. Transforming moments come to our souls through various avenues. Most of us will not have the same kind of experience that Paul had on the Damascus road. Many of us will never hear words like those St. Augustine heard, that encouraged him to, "Take up and read." There are ways, however, to open our souls to transformational possibilities by developing a density of readiness. To believe in God's continuing revelation, which is a basic tenet of the Quaker faith, is to recognize that possibilities for *new* moments of awakening are always before us. These moments give the journey of life meaning, and to live in the expectant rhythm of such moments, is to learn the secret of living in the fullest sense of that word.

Have you experienced what can be described as a "transforming moment" or moments?

In what ways are you developing a density of readiness for an experience of God?

4.

Simmering

Our spirits resound with clashings . . .
While something deep within hungers and
thirsts for the still moment and resting lull.

I LOVE THE WORD *simmering*. It is a word born out of meditative silence but has more to do with life rhythm than with lack
of sound. Something about the word reaches deep into my soul.
This is especially true after times when words like frantic, hurry,
and impatience describe the experiences through which I have just
passed. Simmering is a calming word, a word closely associated
with, if not synonymous with *lingering* or *savoring*.

I first became acquainted with the spiritual meaning of simmering after I read the works of the African American theologian,
Howard Thurman. At a crucial point in my spiritual development,
his writing became an important part of my journey. Thurman
made it a daily discipline to practice what he called, simmering. He
never went directly to sleep when he would lie down, but would
simmer, reflecting on the day's activities and meditating on how he
had experienced God interacting with him. And he never jumped
out of bed in the morning, but simmered, preparing his soul for
the tasks that lay ahead. Thurman further always traveled by train,

whatever his destination. He felt that flying disrupted the rhythms of his life. He writes, "Our spirits resound with clashings, while something deep within hungers and thirsts for the still moment and resting lull." For Howard Thurman, being in tune with the spiritual rhythm of his life was basic to caring for his soul.

In his book, *Fire In The Belly*, Sam Keen describes his first encounter with Howard Thurman at Boston University where he had gone to take one of Thurman's classes: "The first day of the seminar, Howard Thurman, then Dean of Marsh Chapel, arrived in class, a large black man with three prominent bumps on his forehead and a habit of silence so deep that it quieted everyone with whom he came in contact. He sat on the edge of the table for an eternity or so, not saying a word, looking at the dozen members of the class, I mean, really looking. Finally, in a slow rich voice, he began to read from Admiral Byrd's account of being alone and near death at the North Pole. When he finished, he paused and asked, 'If you were alone, a thousand miles from any other person, it was fifty degrees below zero, and you were dying, what would have to have happened to allow you to die with integrity and with a sense of completion?' The question dropped down beneath all the manufactured certainties of my mind and exploded in my gut like a depth charge. I knew I was in the presence of a man who thought with his mind, heart and body stretched to their fullest."

At a certain point in life's journey, simmering becomes more attractive. The activism of youth rarely understands, nor can it relate to what it means to try and live life from a simmering perspective. And some cultures can be very distracting to the idea of simmering, North America being the chief culprit. In recent years, I find that I am more inclined to seek times to simmer.

When I was a younger man, I was a long-distance runner. These days I am a long-distance walker. I miss my days of running, but walking has given me much needed times for simmering. *Simmering walks*, as I have come to call them, are wonderful opportunities to reflect on the day's activities and my relational encounters. Some queries I ask myself as I walk include: "Am I using the sacred gift of time today in a meaningful way?" "Have

I been helpful in lifting human burdens today?" "Have I been an encourager to those in need of encouragement?" "What spiritual lessons am I learning from today's experiences?" As I walk, I think of those I love and pray for them. I also think of those who need extra grace, and who can be spiritually de-energizing to me, and pray for them. On occasion I physically lift my arms and wrap certain persons in the Light, lifting them to God.

Simmering is a means to help a person understand his or her life rhythm, and to stay connected to the spiritual aspirations within the soul. In a world filled with anxiety, terrorism, continuous war, and sadness, simmering can be soul saving. I am grateful for my Quaker faith and the practice of silence that leads to simmering. And I am grateful to Howard Thurman for providing a practical example of how simmering can help me understand the rhythm of my soul.

In what ways have you practiced
the spiritual discipline of simmering?

Are you aware of the rhythm of your soul?
Are you careful not to disturb this rhythm?

5.

The Drama Within

Within the silences of the souls of persons,
an eternal drama is ever being enacted.

I HAVE NEVER LIVED in a time when our nation has experienced so much fearful anxiety. Each day is filled with anxiety raising issues: threats of a government shutdown, long time inhabitants of this country, good, hard working people, continuously threatened with deportation, foreign interference in our elections, wars and rumors of wars, scientific evidence of global warming ignored, expressions of racism openly flaunted, and fears over what some claim as the "deep state." These issues, and many more, haunt our daily lives and our dreams at night. Is there something, anything that we can do to provide hope and relief from the tension and stress that is so widespread?

Thomas Kelly penned the words that I have chosen as an epigraph to this volume. He is an author that I frequently quote, and apart from the Bible, his book, *A Testament of Devotion*, is the book I turn to most often for spiritual guidance. "Out in front of us," writes Kelly, "is the drama of people and of nations, seething, struggling, laboring and dying. Upon this tragic drama in these days our eyes are all set in anxious watchfulness and in prayer.

But within the silences of the souls of persons, an eternal drama is ever being enacted, in these days as well as in others. And on the outcome of this inner drama, rests, ultimately, the outer pageant of history."

On the outcome of this inner drama rests, ultimately, the outer pageant of history. These words from Kelly, a Quaker Philosophy Professor from Haverford College, were penned during World War II, the greatest calamity of the twentieth century. Kelly had the insight and experience of God within his own heart to recognize that the outer pageant of history depends upon the inner drama within each soul.

During this tense and anxiety-filled time in our world, it is important that we remind ourselves of the drama within each of us, and how that drama affects the drama being played out in the "outer pageant of history." What are some of the marks of this inner drama about which Thomas Kelly so eloquently wrote? In my own life, there are at least two major acts to this drama.

The first act has to do with coming to terms with my issues of *power and control.* The Bible and other great spiritual writings through the centuries have a fundamentally different understanding of power than the world's understanding of power. The world worships the power in money, influence, control, prestige, and status. The symbols of God's power, however, as expressed in spiritual writings throughout history, have to do with spiritual risk-taking for those who are poor, hungry and thirsty, and being the voice for persons who are being treated unjustly and living on the fringe of our society.

I have sadly watched many clergy succumb to the lure of worldly power. Money, prestige, and influence in the powerful circles of government have been a huge temptation to these ministers of the Gospel. Called to be a servant to one who called himself a servant, many ministers of the gospel have become the *served.*

A large church in the South invited me to deliver a series of messages during Lent. On Sunday morning, I spoke at the early worship service and again later in the morning. Between worship services, the senior minister invited me to his study. Sitting beside his desk, the minister "buzzed" his personal servant, and asked him to bring us some coffee. Within five minutes the minister's butler, complete with white jacket, appeared in the study with a silver tray and cups of coffee. The minister dismissed the butler by saying, "That will be all," and bowing politely, the butler backed out of the study. It was an amazing experience, and one that I do not normally have when I am invited to be a guest speaker. Usually someone shows me where the plastic cups are and points me to the coffee maker!

It is easy to enjoy such comforts, and it is easy to succumb to the temptation to worldly power. Whenever we have fallen prey to these temptations, human history does not serve us well. In the name of service to God, European nations launched the crusades, inquisitions were organized, Native Americans were enslaved, and much moral manipulation has been engaged in.

Confronting the issues of power and control is a huge part of the drama going on within me, and I am sure within many others. A second act of this inner drama has to do with *the search for wholeness in my spiritual life.* For me, this means maintaining a tension of growth between four dyads: First is *relationship and aloneness.* Quakers represent a faith of one another. One of our testimonies is community. But the Quaker faith also values the mystical tradition of aloneness. The wholeness I seek is a balance between being with others in community and being alone to meditate and pray.

Another dyad of wholeness for me is *thinking and feeling.* As someone has truly said, "The greatest distance a person will travel is the twelve inches from the head to the heart." For those of us most comfortable in the emotional and feeling side of spirituality, however, a journey from the heart to the head can be just as long. To balance my love of God with both mind and heart helps my journey toward wholeness.

A third dyad is *restlessness and contentment.* Both a sense of restlessness and contentment are important to my spiritual growth. And for the most part, I do not choose to be restless! Experientially, I know that restlessness will come as a by-product of pain and struggle. In the movie, *Shadowlands*, Jack (the author C.S. Lewis, played by Anthony Hopkins) and Joy (Lewis's wife played by Debra Winger) are walking in the Golden Valley in England. Joy has cancer but is temporarily in remission. She tells Jack, "We must talk about it, about my dying." Jack is reluctant to talk about her death during such a wonderful walk. But Joy insists, "We must talk about it, Jack. You see, *the pain then is a part of the happiness now.* (Emphasis mine) That is the deal." Throughout my life, I have learned to be thankful to God for both pain and restlessness, as well as for the times of contentment when I can live out the lessons learned during these restless experiences.

Finally, there is the dyad of *Mystery and Belief.* To know the Living God and experience the Light Within, we must be comfortable in mystery. The other day I was on a gym treadmill, and the television nearby was tuned to a religious station. As I worked out, a man on the TV used a piece of chalk and a blackboard to explain God's plan for each of us. (He was an older man, and so I figured that he was not acquainted with power point!) He droned on and on, and I finally stopped on the treadmill and stared at the mass of chalky diagrams filling the screen, from circles to boxes, with arrows all around. I thought to myself, I wish that I could be as sure about *anything* as this man is about *everything*! The TV evangelist was trying to do the impossible. He was trying to capture God via chalk diagram.

On the other hand, belief is an important aspect of spiritual growth, and needs to be held in tandem with mystery. My Earlham School of Religion theology professor would say, "I believe in the mystery of God, but not too soon!" Learning to be comfortable in the tension between mystery and belief is to be on a quest for wholeness.

By working on my own issues of power and control, and by working to live my life in the tension of the many aspects of spiritual wholeness, my inner drama is playing out. And this drama within, about which Thomas Kelly has written, is forever being enacted in all of us: "And on the outcome of this inner drama rests, ultimately, the outer pageant of history."

Has your anxiety been raised over what you are experiencing in our country and world?

What are the spiritual issues of your inner drama?

Part II.

COMMUNITY AND RELATIONSHIP

6.

Mystery and Community

I don't know, I don't know . . . It may be.

HOWARD THURMAN CONCLUDED HIS sermons by saying, "I don't know, I don't know . . . It may be." In closing this way, Thurman left his hearers with much to contemplate. Long after the thoughts in the sermon might be forgotten, the depth of the speaker's humility would be remembered. *It may be.*

Humility. A spiritual quality that we could use more of these days. We are living in a time when too many people seem more and more certain of their opinions and beliefs, with precious little room in their minds and conversation for doubt. Apparently, the more often and the more loudly people proclaim their beliefs, the more their hearers will become convinced of its truth. Raising questions, looking at possible exceptions or maintaining a healthy level of doubt toward one's assumptions, are rarely evident in today's public discourse.

Why is there an ever-increasing cacophony of certitudes that paralyze discourse? Why have so many of our minds and hearts closed to any challenge put forth by those who disagree with our beliefs?

I suggest that one reason is our discomfort with *mystery*. Such discomfort has many origins, from the rapid change that we experience every day, thus increasing our hunger for certainty, to the lack of time for reflective thought when we can muse, simmer, and question our stated beliefs. It seems to me that if we are to know *Truth*, we should learn to be comfortable in the mystery that surrounds us. This is especially true of the religious seeker. No matter how much we try to define God and systematize our process of knowing, there will always be mystery beyond our knowledge.

I was a young boy when I first heard the words of the seventeenth century Quaker theologian, Robert Barclay. Sitting in the silence of the Minneapolis Friends Meeting, I heard my father quote the following words many times as he spoke out of the quiet: "Not by strength of arguments or by a particular disquisition of each doctrine and convincement of my understanding thereby, came I to receive and bear witness of the Truth, but by *secretly* being reached by the Life . . . For when I came into the silent assemblies of God's people, I felt a *secret* power among them, which touched my heart, and as I gave way unto it, I found the evil weakening in me, and the good raised up."

"Secretly being reached by the Life . . ." And "I felt a secret power among them . . ." Barclay uses the word "secret" or "secretly" twice in this brief description of his experience. It seems an odd use of the word, and yet it is, perhaps, the only way that he could describe what had touched his soul so profoundly. It is to acknowledge the awesome mystery of God. Not the kind of mystery or secret associated with a God who loomed high above the human race in a faraway heaven, but, instead, a "secret power" which was *felt* in this earthly realm, and which could actually move one to *feel* the "evil weakening" and "the good raised up."

To accept the truth that mystery surrounds us is to accept our human frailty and admit with the apostle Paul that we do, indeed, "see through a mirror dimly." The more we grow spiritually and come to know the Living God, the more we will become comfortable with mystery, and recognize that there is so much more to learn.

Another reason for today's cacophony of certitudes may be a focus on individualism, that overshadows the importance of a diverse community that lovingly challenges our certitudes. We are a nation of individuals. There is little within our national tradition that emphasizes community. This individualism has been with American culture since its beginning and involves giving priority to the concerns of the individual's life and fulfillment, over a concern for the whole of our society. For instance, note the national debate over gun ownership. How many mass shootings by unstable people does a society tolerate before we re-examine the second amendment to the Constitution? Within the realm of religious faith, this involves giving priority to individual spiritual needs over the mission of the faith community.

Both a private life and communal life are basic to an individual's spiritual growth. Many observers of contemporary faith and society, however, believe that there is a growing tendency to give individuals priority over community. Many Americans view their religious involvement in meeting, church, synagogue or mosque, as a journey among individuals rather than a community moving together.

We need one another to help check and balance our belief systems, as well as the certitudes we express. Anna Quindlen wrote an article titled, *Life of the Closed Mind*, in which she ponders, "Is that true? Maybe I should change my mind? When was the last time you can remember a public dialogue that followed that useful discourse?" I hope that as we work out the faith by which we live within the beloved community, such a dialogue will always be open to us.

Learning to be comfortable in mystery, as well as being a part of a diverse faith community that challenges our certitudes, seems to be a healthy way to go about the process of spiritual growth. I believe that in this process, we will also recover that most important spiritual virtue, *humility*. Columnist George Will offers words that can be applied to all areas of public discourse: "America is currently awash in an unpleasant surplus of clanging, clashing certitudes. It has been well said that the spirit of liberty is the spirit of not being too sure that you are right. One way to immunize ourselves against misplaced certitude is to contemplate, even savor, the strangeness of everything, including ourselves." *I don't know, I don't know, it may be.*

> *Do you keep your God in a box of certitudes, or are you open to God's unfathomable mystery?*
>
> *Do you test your certainties with others who may disagree with you? With your faith community?*

7.

On What Can We Agree?

Compassion is the wellspring of religion . . .

THAT WE ARE LIVING in a dangerous time is not startling news to most of us. Many issues and culture clashes threaten to undo the fabric of tolerance and diversity that holds our world together. Such issues and clashes are equally prevalent within American religious communities and cultures.

Throughout their history, Quakers have sought to unite in peace the multiple cultures and faith traditions that make up our world. Quakers have a testimony on peace, to which they seek to adhere in times of peace and in times of conflict. They believe in protesting war in all its forms and working diligently for peace in the absence of conflict. A few years ago, the former president of Earlham College in Indiana, Landrum Bolling, a Quaker who worked throughout his life searching for peace in the Middle East, was asked what concerned him most about our world. His response: "The rise of fundamentalism within all of the major faith traditions."

Fundamentalism and extremism have and *will* always be a part of all religious faiths, whether it is a fundamentalism that keeps a strangle hold on traditions that can no longer be reasonably defended, or an extremism that does not respect any other tradition or theological position. Intolerance will always be with us. The best of our religious traditions, however, and the best within each of us, will seek to discover those areas within all major faiths that unite and sustain us, and which provide a basis to understand those who are different.

While I was the minister of faith and learning at Wayzata Community Church in Minnesota, I invited Karen Armstrong, the former nun and now prolific author, to speak about her book, *The Great Transformation: The Beginning of Our Religious Traditions.* Of the many important points she made, none seemed more important than this: "Compassion is the wellspring of religion." She observed that some five-hundred years before Jesus, Confucius expressed the "Golden Rule." It remains the touchstone of all the major faith traditions. As I reflected on Armstrong's observation, I began to consider these questions: Besides the "Golden Rule," what else unites and sustains our different faiths? What are those elements, values, teachings, and truths that we can respect and honor within the Christian tradition, as well as within the tradition of Judaism and Islam? How can these common values lessen the dangerous faith and culture clashes of our time? In brief, without diluting the witness and understanding in Christianity, Judaism and Islam, and recognizing that ours is a diverse world, *on what can we agree?*

At the heart of all three of these major faiths, is a spiritual hunger for connection with the Living God. Mystical elements within these traditions greatly enhance our faiths and our love of and search for the Living God. For example, the writings of St. Francis within the Roman Catholic tradition, who many have considered a "nature mystic." Ilia Delio writes, "Francis has been described as a nature mystic, one who finds God in the vast and beautiful fields of nature. Everything spoke to Francis of the infinite love of God. Trees, worms, lonely flowers by the side of the road, all were saints gazing up into the face of God. In this way, creation became the place to find God, and, in finding God, he realized his intimate relation to all creation." James Nayler and Thomas Kelly, both Quakers, exemplify this mystical element within Christianity. On his death bed, James Nayler said, "There is a Spirit which I feel that delights to do no evil, nor to avenge any wrong, but delights to endure all things, in hope to enjoy its own in the end. Its hope is to outlive all wrath and contention, and to weary out all exaltation and cruelty, or whatever is of a nature contrary to itself." Writing from an inward spiritual place, Kelly wrote, "Deep within us all there is an amazing inner sanctuary of the soul, a holy place, a Divine Center, a speaking Voice to which we may continuously return. Eternity is at our hearts, pressing upon our time-torn lives, warming us with intimations of an astounding destiny, calling us home unto Itself. Yielding to these persuasions, gladly committing ourselves in body and soul, utterly and completely, to the Light Within, is the beginning of true life."

Abraham Heschel from the Jewish tradition defines "spiritual" as the "ecstatic force that stirs all of our goals. When we perceive it, it is as if our mind were gliding awhile with an eternal current." He writes about a religious person as, "one who holds God and humans in one thought at one time, at all times, who suffer harm done to others, whose greatest passion is compassion, whose greatest strength is love and defiance of despair."

Finally, the poet, Rumi, representing the Sufi Muslim tradition has declared, "Look at spirit how it fuses with earth giving it new life . . . the wolf and lamb, the lion and deer far away yet together . . . Looking at the unity of this spring and winter manifested in the equinox . . ." All these writers from their various traditions are evidence of a mystic hunger for and experience with the Living God which can serve to unite and sustain us.

Justice is also at the core of all faiths. Jim Wallis of *Sojourners* Magazine has noted that archaeologists, in peeling away the layers of dirt in their digs in Israel, have been able to discern those periods when the prophets of Israel were most active and vocal by recognizing where there is the greatest discrepancy between the very rich and the very poor. Jesus made issues of justice the heart of his teaching, proclaiming that neglect of those who are hungry, thirsty, naked, sick, and in prison, is a rejection of him.

Muhammad's message was first greeted with hostility by those in the culture where he lived, when he preached an uncompromising monotheism, an end to licentiousness and a challenge to the unjust social order. Indeed, one of the five pillars of Islam addresses the disparity of wealth in the world and admonishes those who have much to help lift the burden of those less fortunate. At core, all major faith traditions are concerned with justice, especially for the poor.

A community that is built on the values of truth and integrity is also at the core of these faith traditions. Ethical conduct within the cultures where we reside concerns all religions. To cheat a brother or sister, or to build a life upon a web of lies, is unacceptable in Christianity, Judaism, and Islam. The words Muhammad spoke during his "farewell pilgrimage" to Mecca and shortly before his death, sound as if they had been written by the apostle Paul in one of his letters to the young Christian churches: "O men! Listen to my words and take them to heart! Know ye that every Muslim is a brother to every other Muslim, and that you are now one brotherhood." These words echo Paul's emphasis upon belonging to one another in Christian community and are certainly a part of the traditional emphasis within the covenantal community of Israel, especially as expressed in Leviticus 19:18, "love your neighbor as yourself."

When an audience participant asked Karen Armstrong what we can do to help bring together today's Christians, Muslims and Jews, she said, "We should not talk about what we believe. We must go beyond 'tolerance' and 'dialogue' and *work* together. We must let our actions show what we believe, what we hold in common." An experiential connection with the Living God, justice for all, and community built upon the values of love, truth, and integrity. These are all important and uniting beliefs of the major faith traditions.

While living in Minnesota, I belonged to a small group that drafted a statement in a concrete practical effort to focus on those things that unite all people. We hoped that our statement would find support in churches, synagogues, and mosques, as we sought ways to work together. In simplicity and brevity, the statement reads: "We come together in our interdependent world of many races, cultures and faith traditions, to learn from one another in peace. Respecting our differences, we seek a better life helping others as we would like to be helped."

Are there other points on which the major faiths agree?

What can you do, and what can your community of faith do to work together to bring peace to the world and unite the various faith cultures?

8.

The Redemptive Community

Therefore encourage one another
and build one another up . . .

Since being welcomed into the community of Oriental, North Carolina, a sailing community where my wife, Elizabeth, and I have a home, I have acquired a nickname. Among those in North Carolina who have known me as just "Jim" rather than "The Reverend Doctor James R. Newby," I am referred to as "Captain Crunch." I was first given this name by one of the persons who was on board my boat when I attempted to dock it. Use of the nickname has become so widespread that I am now receiving emails addressed to "Captain Crunch." You would think that there would be a greater element of grace within the boating community there, and that a few bumps or crunches against the dock or other boats could be more easily forgiven. Not so. The name is sticking, despite my reassuring pleas that any dentist can repair rattled fillings in teeth, and broken limbs will heal over time!

Community. It is that place where people know you, I mean, *really know you.* It is where we can playfully tease one another and laugh at our human foibles, of which there are many, including boat docking abilities. A redemptive community is where we come to understand our responsibility to one another, and where we express our love to others by inviting them into community with us.

The folk-singer John McCutcheon once performed a concert at Plymouth Church in Des Moines, Iowa, where I served as the minister of spiritual growth. He spoke about the hit television program, *Survivor*, and exclaimed, "We don't survive by voting people out of community. We survive by welcoming people into community!" Community is one of our Quaker testimonies, which means that it has played an important part in my personal spiritual development.

What makes a community *redemptive*? I suggest that a redemptive community is one that encourages the processing of one another's pain. We are all wounded in one way or another, and pain needs to be processed and expressed. I believe that in community such processing can best happen.

Mary Cosby, who was one of the founders of the Church of the Savior in Washington, DC, has told the story of a new minister in her mother's church in Georgia. Mary's mother, if she was a Quaker, would be considered a "weighty Friend." The new pastor asked her, "If you could say one thing to me before I enter the pulpit of our church for the first time this Sunday, what would you say?" With little hesitation, Mary's mother responded, "Each time that you look out on that congregation, and into the eyes of each person there, remember that each is sitting beside his or her own pool of tears." Each of us has a pool of tears. Some pools are deeper than others, but each of us has such a pool. Within the redemptive community this pain can be eased by sharing it with others.

Another important component of a redemptive community is that it must be a place to encourage one another. Our interactions in the world can be negative and critical. Within the redemptive community, however, there is no room for hurtful criticism. In every community of faith where I have served, I have focused my ministry on a verse from the apostle Paul's First Letter to the Church at Thessalonica, "Therefore encourage one another and build one another up." (5:11)

In the movie *Zorba the Greek*, there is an exchange between an old neighbor and the main character, Alexis: "One day he took me on his knee and placed his hand on my hand as though he were giving me his blessing. 'Alexis,' he said, 'I am going to tell you a secret. You're too small to understand now, but you'll understand when you are bigger. Listen, little one, neither the seven stories of heaven nor the seven stories of earth are enough to contain God; but a person's heart can contain Him. So be very careful, Alexis, and may my blessing go with you, *never to wound a person's heart.*'" And yet we do wound the hearts of others, often unintentionally. Within a redemptive community, the focus is on encouraging one another.

The redemptive community is also that place where we come to know and to nurture our spiritual experiences. There is a hunger within me, and seems to be in many others, for an experience with God that is personal, not remote, an experience that moves me emotionally, not merely intellectually.

The plea to make God "personal" was the impetus for Marcus Borg to write his best-selling book, *Meeting Jesus Again for the First Time*. Borg recounted being asked to speak before an Episcopal men's group: "Because of the nature of the group," he writes, "their instructions were two-fold . . . Talk to us about Jesus and make it *personal.*" I believe that with so much emphasis upon ritual and debate over peripheral issues, as well as the cumbersome work of institutional religion, we are experiencing a surge of interest in a personal, experiential spirituality.

My father, a Quaker minister, would often tell the story about the tourists from the Midwest being guided through London's Westminster Abbey. The guide had spoken for about an hour concerning architecture and the beauty of the windows, as well as telling about the historical figures buried there. Finally, a woman in the group interrupted the guide, asking, "This is all very well, young man, but has anyone been *saved* here lately?" Although her language may not speak to you spiritually, this woman knew how to move from a focus on mere tradition to a focus on the spiritually significant. Spiritual significance is rooted and centered in a personal relationship with the Living God, and the redemptive community nurtures such a relationship.

Community is also that place to find unconditional love and find reassurance that for all our shortcomings we are *all right* in the eyes of our fellow spiritual pilgrims and our God. Watching the movie, *Saving Private Ryan* has become part of an annual ritual for me each June 6, the anniversary of D-Day. The film is about a group of World War II soldiers who were sent on a mission to find a Private Ryan and send him home. All of Ryan's brothers had been killed in the war. He was the only surviving son. Toward the end of the movie, the officer in charge of the group, a character played by Tom Hanks, is shot and dying. Most of his company of soldiers have already been killed or seriously wounded. Ryan, however, survives, and as he leans over Hanks to try and stop his bleeding, Hanks looks up and begs, "Ryan, make this worth it." Then he dies.

The movie's epilogue shows Ryan, fifty years older, standing over the grave in France of Hanks' character. Ryan's wife is with him, and with tears in his eyes, he looks at her and pleads, "Tell me I have been a good man! Tell me that I am a good man!"

Ryan's plea to his wife is one that we repeat throughout our lives. All of us need the reassurance that we are "okay," that we are doing the good as best we know how. In the redemptive community, we find the unconditional love of reassurance, a love that lets us know that with all our faults and human sins, we are *okay*.

At a seminar I attended led by the Quaker author Parker Palmer, he defined community as "that place where the person you least want to be with is always present." He then added, "And when that person leaves or dies, there is always someone else to take his or her place!" The important point that Palmer wants us to understand is that in this world of imperfection, we will never find the perfect community. As much as we would like to be soul mates with all persons within our community, that is impossible. There will always be someone who irritates us and who is socially inept with others. Learning to love and work with such persons is a part of what community is about.

When I teach classes on Quakerism, I share a warning to all those who are considering membership in Cincinnati Friends Meeting. In brief, I explain that meetings are not perfect institutions, and neither are the members who fill the benches on First Day Morning, who staff its committees or work to bring to life the testimonies that we hold in common. What does this mean? It means that if you are a part of this meeting, one of two things will eventually happen. One, you will disappoint the meeting, or two, the meeting will disappoint you. The time may come when the meeting doesn't do something that you believe is vitally important. We may fail to act on an issue or even act in a manner contrary to what you expect. At the same time, it is possible you might *not* do something that the meeting asks of you or do it in a way that does not meet the expectations of other members. These disappointments are inevitable within a community of faith. Though such inevitable disappointments are sad, it is a part of being *imperfect* people banding together in an *imperfect* way to create an *imperfect* institution.

The redemptive community: A place of imperfect people where we *process our pain and the pain of others*, where we *encourage one another and build up one another,* where we *come to know, experientially, the Living God,* and where we are *loved unconditionally, knowing that for all our short comings, we are still "okay."* And one more thing: a redemptive community is that place where *we learn to love and live with one another*, regardless of how irritating and obnoxious others can be.

Do you belong to a redemptive community?
How important is such a community to your spiritual life?

9.

Agreeing to Differ . . .
Resolving to Love

Here we enter a fellowship.
Sometimes we will agree to differ,
but always we will resolve
to love and unite to serve.

MY FATHER THOUGHT THAT Hubert Humphrey was one
of the greatest men who ever lived. He had worked with then
Mayor Humphrey in the 1950s, serving with him on the Human
Relations Council in Minneapolis. Ever since, he had followed with
great interest Humphrey's political career. I did not know Hubert
Humphrey prior to his time as vice-president under President
Lyndon Johnson. And I was not nearly as fond of him as my father
was. I was a freshman in college in 1968 when Humphrey decided
to run for the presidency.

Also running for president was a Minnesota Senator named
Eugene McCarthy. I liked him in 1968. He represented a change
from the past and was popular with young people. As these men
debated the Vietnam War and other important issues, they also
set the stage for a debate in the Newby household. To make things

even more interesting, my grandmother, who was living with us at the time, was an ardent supporter of Richard Nixon. After all, he was a Quaker, and my grandmother felt that we should support "one of our own." Our home was not a pleasant place to eat dinner. Inevitably, someone would raise the subject of politics each time we sat down at the table together.

"And for this food, we give Thee thanks. Amen." "Dad, did you hear what McCarthy said today?" "I heard that Richard Nixon has a secret plan to end the War." "If we just let Hubert run his own show, he will be a terrific president." I'm not sure of the order of such comments, but they were all there. From the moment the prayer of thanksgiving ended, until the last bite of dessert, politics dominated mealtime.

As I reflect on those family meals, I cannot help but smile. There we were, one middle-class family carrying the weight of the world's problems on our shoulders. We really did love one another beyond our differing political beliefs, and I suppose that during such times together I learned how to differ with someone over religion and politics, while at the same time respecting and loving the person behind the belief. Many years later, I read the words of Robert Owen, founder of the utopian community of New Harmony, Indiana, and remembered those dinner discussions: "If we cannot reconcile all opinions, let us endeavor to unite all hearts." This is not to say that our verbal exchanges did not skirt the boundary of human respect. They did. In the end, however, we knew that we were still family and that our hearts were united in love.

A few years ago, I attended a seminar based on the work of M. Scott Peck on the deteriorating state of civility in America. The loss of civility shows up most clearly in our society's discussions of faith and political issues, but within a meeting or church incivility could arise over any number of things! We have reached the point where we no longer listen to one another but instead, see who can debate his or her point of view the most loudly. Talk radio and cable news are famous for this kind of lack of civility, but it has infiltrated all segments of our lives. Our problems are beyond being Republican or Democrat, Baptist or Roman Catholic, Quaker or Presbyterian. The problems are *spiritual*. We care more about winning a discussion, and/or argument, than *caring* for the person with the different point of view.

Dehumanizing someone or some group that we do not know is temptingly easy. I recently shared a posting on Facebook about immigrants, dispelling the untruths that have been circulating and challenging the negative words that have recently been used against them. Here is one of the responses I received from a friend I knew in high school: "The truth about migrants, legal or not, is that they bring diseases back to America that have been eradicated for years. Most turn to a life of crime because they do not speak English. If a person wants to live in America, they should learn English." Fox News could not have said it better. My response to this posting was simple: "My wife is a migrant." (See her book, *A Migrant with Hope in a Time of Despair*) We can all think of times we would like to take back our words. I am sure that my friend from high school had no idea that I had married a Hispanic migrant woman, and if he could change his reply to my post he probably would. What we say matters. Words matter.

Throughout the M. Scott Peck seminar on civility, we interacted with each other, telling our stories. We talked about the major faith events in our lives that were *teachable* or *awakening*. We discussed the political events that shaped us. Instead of asking, "*What* do you believe?" we asked, "*Why* do you believe?" In the two days of the seminar, we came to understand each other in a civilized way, rather than hurling our points of view at each other.

To share with one another in a civil way, certain elements must underlie our life together. The first element is *trust*. Perhaps the most trusting figure in American popular culture is Charlie Brown, the comic strip character created by Charles Schulz. Those familiar with Charlie Brown and the *Peanuts'* characters can remember the many episodes featuring Charlie Brown, Lucy, and a football. Lucy challenges Charlie Brown to kick the ball while she holds it. Charlie is sure that Lucy will pull the ball away just as he tries to kick it, and he will end up flat on his back. He says to her, "You must think I am crazy. You say that you will hold the

ball, but you won't. You will pull it away and I'll break my neck."
With the look of an angel, Lucy responds with a wide smile, "Why
Charlie Brown, how you talk! I wouldn't think of such a thing. I
am a changed person. Look, isn't this a face you can trust?" Since
Charlie Brown is Charlie Brown, he accepts Lucy at her word. "All
right, you hold the ball and I'll come running up and kick it." Sure
enough, the expected happens, and as Charlie flies to the ground,
he can only shout, "She did it again!" In the last scene, Lucy is
leaning over Charlie to say, "I admire you Charlie Brown. You have
such faith in human nature."

In a sense, our whole society is built on the kind of trust that
Charlie Brown displays. Civility is not possible without *trust*.

The art of *listening* is also important to civil discourse. During that state of civility seminar I attended, two or three of us sat
together and listened to one another. Each person had three minutes to speak, and the rule was that no one could interrupt. This
is not as easy as it sounds! In our day of talking at each other and
short attention spans, patient, attentive listening to one another
is a very difficult discipline. And yet, if our society is to recover
civility, it is necessary.

A third element helpful in the recovery of civility is *vulnerability*. To be open and vulnerable, letting our defenses down as
we interact with one another, will help us be more civil, and it will
help us to grow spiritually.(See chapter 19) The more open and
vulnerable we become, and the more authentic we can be with others, the more civil our discourse will be.

On the wall in my study hangs the motto of Plymouth Church
in Des Moines, Iowa. It reads, "We agree to differ . . . We resolve to
love . . . We unite to serve." These words are a part of a larger saying
that was displayed over the ashram in India of the American Mis-
sionary, E. Stanly Jones: "Here we enter a fellowship. Sometimes
we will agree to differ, but always we will resolve to love and unite
to serve." A fellowship or a society that agrees to differ but resolves
to love one another will be a community incorporating the elements of *trust*, *listening*, and *vulnerability*. At times we will fail, but
then we begin again. To live together requires nothing less.

What are some ways and settings wherein you can practice the disciplines of trust, listening, and vulnerability?

What must change within you so that you can become more civil with others?

10.

Relationship and Story

Piglet sidled up to Pooh from behind. "Pooh,"
he whispered. "Yes, Piglet?" "Nothing,"
said Piglet, reaching for Pooh's paw,
"I just wanted to be sure of you."

RELATIONSHIPS ARE AT THE heart of spiritual growth. I consider myself a *relational theologian*, which means that I experience God in other persons. I believe that *much of the meaning of human life can be found in that awkward dance between our yearning for relationship, and the need to discover our individuality.* This chapter focuses on our yearning for relationship.

As I do for so many spiritual profundities, I turn to the medium of story. Specifically, I am grateful to what have been labeled "Children's Stories," for the meaningful way they can provide insights into the human condition. For my focus on relationships, I am helped by the wisdom found in *The Velveteen Rabbit, Charlotte's Web,* and *Winnie-the-Pooh.*

From *The Velveteen Rabbit* there are these words: "'What is *real,*' asked the Rabbit one day. 'Does it mean having things that buzz inside of you and a stick-out handle?' 'Real isn't about how you are made,' said the Skin Horse. 'It's a thing that happens to you.

When a child loves you for a long, long time, not just to play with, but *really* loves you, then you become *real*.'

"'Does it hurt,' inquired the Rabbit. 'Sometimes,' said the Skin Horse, for he was always truthful. 'When you are *real* you don't mind being hurt.' The Rabbit continues his questioning: 'Does it happen all at once, like being wound up, or bit by bit?'

"'It doesn't happen all at once,' responded the Skin Horse, 'You become. It takes a long time. That is why it doesn't often happen to people who break easily, or who have sharp edges, or who have to be carefully kept. Generally, by the time you are *real*, most of your hair has been loved off, and your eyes drop out and you get loose in the joints and very shabby. But these things don't matter at all, because once you are *real* you can't be ugly, except to people who don't understand.'"

In life together, in our relationships with one another, being *real* is of central importance. I do not want to be in relationship with persons who are not *real*, who are phony and pretentious. To be *real* means that we are honest with one another, and open with one another about our failings and successes. In short, I want to be in relationships where I can share my sorrows without fear and celebrate my joys openly.

While I was going through a divorce, I received a call from a former student. He was angry that I was divorcing and that I had failed him and others who looked up to me. I let him speak, and then at the end of his scolding, I said, "You know, Bob, staying on that pedestal where you placed me took way too much of my spiritual and emotional energy. I' m sorry to be such a disappoint to you." What my wife and I were experiencing together throughout our divorce, (We eventually remarried) was the growth process described by the Skin Horse to the Rabbit. We were becoming *real*. For my wife Elizabeth and I, it was radical relationship surgery, but we would not change what we went through. We became *real* to one another.

In the book, *Charlotte's Web*, Charlotte expresses her great admiration for Wilbur. Remember, Charlotte is a spider, and Wilbur is a pig. Charlotte spelled out the word *terrific* in her web above the pigpen where Wilbur lived: "Wilbur blushed, 'but I am not *terrific*, Charlotte. I am just about average for a pig.' 'You're *terrific* as far as I am concerned,' replied Charlotte, 'and that is what counts. You are my best friend, and I think you are sensational.'"

A vital part of all relationships is the feeling that the ones with whom we are in relationship believe that we are *terrific*. The world is filled with challenges that can bring us down, times when we do not quite measure up. To the world beyond our closest relationships, we may be just an "average pig," but within the circle of those who truly love us, we should always feel like we are *terrific*.

And there is this bit of relationship wisdom from Piglet in *Winnie-the-Pooh*: "Piglet sidled up to Pooh from behind. 'Pooh,' he whispered. 'Yes Piglet?' 'Nothing,' said Piglet, reaching for Pooh's paw, 'I just wanted to be *sure* of you.'"

In our closest relationships, we need to feel *sure* of each other. We need to be able to count on one another and to trust one another. When we make promises, we need to be *sure* that we keep those promises. To be *sure* of someone is to believe that whatever happens in this life, there will always be someone, somewhere who loves us and will support us. This assurance is unconditional.

The Inner Light shines in the eyes of others. To be in relationship is to experience and to know the Living God. The most intimate of these relationships requires us to be *real*, to believe that the other is *terrific*, and to know that we can trust and feel *sure* with that person or persons. I am grateful to Rabbit and Skin Horse, Charlotte and Wilbur, and Piglet and Pooh for their ability to express what is in my heart.

What spiritual lessons have you learned
in your relationships?

What other stories express what is
important in relationships?

Part III.

PAIN AND GROWTH

11.

The Rhythms of Life

Where did I go?

A YOUNG BOY'S PARENTS were taking him through the "potty training" stage of development. One evening the little fellow came to his father, tugged on his pant leg, and let him know in no uncertain terms that he needed to be taken to the nearest bathroom. All parents who have been through this process know that when your child says, "It is time," you do not wait to finish your sentence; you go right away!

The facility to which the father escorted his son was just off the kitchen, which had no window for outside light. The only source of illumination was controlled by an electrical switch outside the door. After the father had placed the little fellow on the seat, the father turned, closed the door, and inadvertently turned off the light. After a brief period of silence, a voice cried from behind the closed door, "Where did I go?!"

As we move along the path of life and spiritual growth, we will inevitably ask the same question, "Where did I go?" Earlier in our development, life looked like a straight shot. No impediments. No detours. Along the way, however, things change. Plans made get thwarted by an unexpected turn of events. People with whom

49

we have planned and with whom we have worked side by side, die too soon. Relationships that seemed solid, fall apart. Promises that felt sure and solid, are not kept. The only thing that is sure, is that life is *not* sure.

All of life is change and movement and tends to fluctuate between degrees of discontent and content. The path of spiritual growth is lined with pain and struggle. I believe that in those times of greatest discontent, we can experience the greatest spiritual growth. To be discontented is to know the working of a God of process and movement deep within one's soul.

Like all things opposite, only through the experience of being discontent can we appreciate and understand fully the feeling of content. My experience has been that the Inner Light nudges, provokes, shoves, and finally blasts us out of old life patterns that are no longer adequate to help us grow spiritually. This same Light, however, also helps us in times of contentment to broaden and deepen what we have learned. For the most part, spiritual learning hurts. But following the pain and struggle associated with the classroom of spirituality, there are enclaves or respites into which we move or are moved, where we can be content, at least for awhile. Where the experience of discontent is a time of intense change and growth, to be content is a time of relative calm when we can expand on the lessons learned.

Thomas Kelly wrote about "the inner sanctuary of the soul." These words were written following a major experience of discontent in his life, failing the oral examination for his PhD, at Harvard University. He was an academic, teaching at Haverford in Philadelphia. After this failure, Kelly went into a deep depression so severe his wife feared that he might take his own life. During that months-long time of turmoil, Kelly experienced what can only be described as spiritual transformation. In the days and months following his academic failure and subsequent depression, Kelly reflected on what he had been through, and began to write about it, deepening and broadening his experience of spiritual growth as he wrote. Here is how he began a lecture at Germantown Friends Meeting, his first lecture since his depression and transformation:

"To you in this room who are seekers, to you, young and old who have toiled all night and caught nothing, but who want to launch out into the deeps and let down your nets for a draught, I want to speak as simply, as tenderly, as clearly as I can. For God can be found. There is a last rock for your souls, a resting place of absolute peace and joy and power and radiance and security. There is a Divine Center into which your life can slip, a new and absolute orientation in God, a Center where you live with God and out of which you see all of life through new and radiant vision, tinged with new sorrows and pangs, new joys unspeakable and full of glory."

Contentment followed Kelly's experience of being discontent, and his life was transformed.

"Where did I go?" We don't have to be in a darkened bathroom to ask the question. And only in asking the question, "Where did I go?" can we begin to understand where we are now. In the discontent of pain and struggle, the old self is dying, and a new self is yearning to be born.

I like Thomas Kelly's phrase, "inner sanctuary of the soul." It is a contentment phrase. It speaks of a Center to be discovered within each of us where the Living God can be found and where true contentment resides. If you are in the throes of discontent, remember that the pattern of history shows that you will again be content. Such is the cycle of spiritual growth, and such is the working of the Inner Light within the human condition.

Where are you in your personal cycle of spiritual growth?

Are you discontented? Are you in a time of contentment?
How do you feel during each of these experiences?

12.

Pain and Loss

Love can never lose its own . . .

THERE HAS BEEN A lot of sadness around me lately. A classmate from high school dies suddenly of a heart attack, and a friend succumbs to cancer. Another member of the "Greatest Generation" exits this physical world, leaving a legacy of tradition, commitment, love of family, and love of country. Two dear friends lose their way in their private plane, crashing into the side of a volcano in Costa Rica, and I watch with tears as a friend holds his dying wife, kissing her gently on the cheek as she dies. The last few weeks have been a time of mourning. In my sadness I have thought again of the opening words of *The Road Less Traveled* by M. Scott Peck, "Life is difficult."

I know that I am not alone in my grief. Everyone has or will experience sadness. In this physical life we cannot escape the death of loved ones, sickness, and depression, that jolt us out of familiar patterns and into that fellowship of those who bear the mark of pain. Loss and grief are universal experiences.

When the Wounded Emerge as Healers was the title of a commencement address that Professor Kimberly C. Patton shared with the graduates of Harvard Divinity School. It was published in the

Harvard Divinity Bulletin. In a very helpful way, her words address the question, "What can we learn from the experience of pain?" Looking into the eyes of the graduates, she said, "Even if a broken heart does not lie in your past or present, it awaits you in your future, at some place, at some time when you will almost certainly be unprepared. But in myth, ritual, and in theology, the broken heart is not a regrettable symptom of derailment, but is rather the starting point of anything that matters . . . The religious imagination reveals the broken heart as the very best means to wisdom and growth, even when it disrupts the dreams and goals that have inspired us; even when it scatters the ducks we have so carefully lined up in a row . . ."

I recently met with a group of ministers on the coast of North Carolina. As we came together, all of us knew about the "scattering of ducks that we had so carefully lined up in a row." We dealt with issues surrounding the broken heart. We sought to process our pain with one another and talked about how we might recover our passion for life and ministry. We tried to understand the increasing sense of paradox in our lives, and we shared our life journeys as we sought to understand them within the sacred context that brokenness always reveals. Many of us were learning the hard truth that the religious institutions to which we had given our lives cannot love us back. We were trying to make the chaos of our lives become sacred.

Professor Patton helped us in this quest to understand the meaning of the pain we were experiencing: "It is highly likely that during such brokenhearted, disorienting times, illusions will shatter, old ideas and attachments will be burned up; old ways of being will dissolve; and the one thing or person or way of life we thought we could not live without will be taken from us. These are times when we will learn compassion . . . times when the unbearably wounded will themselves emerge as healers."

A broken heart is not something to be desired; it causes terrible pain. But a broken heart also becomes a softer heart, more aware of the pain of others. If the wounds do not turn to bitterness, wounds in the heart can become a place where God works to bring about tenderness and kindness and move us to compassion. Life is, indeed, an accumulation of scars. Healing our scars is a continuous process of growing in our ability to allow love into our injured hearts. During this time of sadness in my own life, I have reflected upon my faith, and the specific question, "How does my faith sustain me during such brokenness?"

My faith has taught me that we have one another for support during difficult times, a community of love where sorrows are divided. I also believe that there is One who can bring light to my darkness, and who can help to heal the brokenness of my grief. That One is the God whom the apostle Paul called, "The God of comfort," and whom Quakers identify as the "Light." I do not believe that God can give us assurances against grief caused by events along life's journey, but during times of pain my faith teaches me that *God is with me.* Faith in God has not made my life easy, but faith has given me strength to face the broken times in my life, and a beloved community for support.

In trying to understand the mystery of death and the feelings of grief when loved ones die, I have found the words in Kahil Gibran's *The Prophet* to be comforting: "You would know the secret of death. But how shall you find it unless you seek it in the heart of life? The owl whose night-bound eyes are blind unto the day cannot unveil the mystery of light. If you would indeed behold the spirit of death, open your heart wide unto the body of life. For life and death are one, even as the river and the seas are one."

The words of the Quaker poet, John Greenleaf Whittier have been similarly comforting:

Alas for him who never sees
the stars shine through the cypress trees.
Who hopeless lays his dead away,
nor looks to see the breaking day
across the mournful marbles play.
Who hath not learned in hours of faith
the truth that time and sense have known,
that life is ever Lord of death,
and love can never lose its own.

I believe that life is a continuum and that love is the constant. If I believe that God is love and that God is infinite, then I can conclude that love is infinite. I am comforted in my brokenness when I come to understand as the poet Whittier understood, that "love can never lose its own."

During my time of sadness, I feel it is all right to cry and express feelings of abandonment and loss. These tearful expressions help to heal the broken heart. But I can also feel the love and support within a beloved community as I live through my pain. I can know that love is infinite, and that God is walking this path of loss with me. Life in this world is difficult. The One I worship, however, has said, "I have overcome the world."

What have been those times when you have experienced loss and heartache?

How have you been helped during such times?

13.

Suffering and Evil

I saw also that there was . . .
an infinite ocean of light and love,
which flowed over the ocean of darkness.

SUFFERING AND EVIL ARE issues that have both challenged one's faith and/or made one's faith stronger. They also raise a difficult question: "How do we reconcile a loving God with the problem of evil and suffering?" It is a question that has plagued all persons who want to believe in a God of love. Authors have written about it, teachers have taught about it, preachers have preached about it, and you and I have talked about it. A child is hit by a car and killed; a tornado rips through a town causing mass destruction and death; terrorists bomb synagogues, mosques and churches and innocent human beings are killed or critically injured. And we ask, "Where is God?" "How could God allow this to happen?" These are ancient questions and they are modern questions. They are questions that can make or break one's faith.

I once visited with a man who has written extensively about the issues of suffering and evil. Because of his inability to reconcile a God of love with the suffering and evil in the world, he has become an agnostic. This is certainly understandable, and the argument against a loving God in the face of the world's suffering can be made. Other theological positions, however, are possible.

Suffering can be caused by two types of evil. First there is *human evil* that causes suffering through the free-will actions of persons. Throughout human history there are endless examples of what we can label, *man's inhumanity to man*. The Holocaust is the most vivid example of this type of evil in the twentieth century. The crashing of airliners into the Twin Towers in New York City, however, has brought this issue to the forefront of twenty-first century Americans. In an interview that Bill Moyers conducted with Andrew Delbanco, a professor of humanities at Columbia University, just following the attack on the Twin Towers, he asked him to define human evil. Delbanco said, "For me, the best I've been able to do is to recognize and come to terms with the reality that there are human beings who are convinced that there is some higher good, some higher ideal to which their lives should be dedicated, that the pain and suffering of other individuals does not matter. It is the absence of the imaginative sympathy for other human beings. The inability to see your victims as humans. To think of them as instruments or cogs or elements or statistics, but not as human beings." Delbanco went on to say that what 9/11 helped us understand is that evil simmers and lies dormant in the world and in each of us.

A second type of evil can be called *natural evil*. Tornadoes, earthquakes, disease, etc. are all examples of what can be called natural evil. I once had a professor at the Earlham School of Religion who said that if we want to connect with and feel the horrors of natural evil, we should read *The Plague* by Albert Camus. In a powerful way, Camus' writing moves us to live with the inhabitants of a town engulfed with the plague. One passage concerning "All Soul's Day" is especially moving: "All Soul's Day that year was very different from what it had been in former years . . . in the plague year people no longer wished to be reminded of their dead. Because, indeed, they were thinking all too much about them as it was . . . each day was for us a Day of the Dead." On the last page of the book, the main character, Dr. Rieux, is listening to the surviving inhabitants of the town celebrate the end of the plague: ". . . as he listened to the cries of joy rising from the town, Rieux remembered that such joy is always imperiled. He knew that those jubilant crowds did not know but could have learned from books: that the plague bacillus never dies or disappears for good; that it can lie dormant for years and years in furniture and linen-chests; that it bides its time in bedrooms, cellars, trunks, and bookshelves; and that perhaps the day would come when, for the bane and the enlightening of men, it would rouse up its rats again and send them forth to die in a happy city."

How do we resolve or reconcile the problem of evil with the belief about a good and loving God? Why would God allow evil and suffering to happen? The tendency is to say, either God does not care, or God is not able to make a difference. Either God is lacking in concern, or God is lacking in power.

I am grateful to my mentor, Elton Trueblood, for many things. His friendship and care for me and my family, for sure, but I am most grateful for the many conversations we had about issues surrounding the areas of philosophy and theology. Every morning that we worked together (I was his associate for fifteen-years) I would sit with this voluminous author and professor of philosophy and we would have these wonderful conversations that challenged my mind and heart. One of the many issues that we discussed was evil and suffering. On one occasion he pointed me to a lecture that he had given on this topic at the founding of the Yokefellow Academy. In summary, here are the points made by this Christian philosopher:

1. Christ, in revealing God to us does not promise us easy lives. He does not say that all our burdens, pains, illnesses and suffering will be taken away. In the Garden of Gethsemane, he prayed, "Oh God, if it be your will, take this cross from me." And he was crucified, and he died. Now, this is not the end of the story, but it is important to understand that the Christian faith is not dependent upon an easy success story, but upon the cross.

2. The pain and suffering that comes from evil can be redemptive. There are numerous instances throughout history where a person has suffered, or a whole community has suffered, and that person or community has been able to lift other people and communities by the quality of life shown in response to pain. It is important to acknowledge that the most effective lives, lives that have touched us most profoundly, are *not* those in which everything is free of pain. Pain, bad as it is, can, under certain circumstances, be redemptive.

3. We must contend with our own ignorance. We do not see very much. As the apostle Paul said, "We see through a glass darkly," and so we cannot know. This is the answer that came to Job. His conclusion is that we see too little in order to be able to make a total judgment.

4. Evil is the necessary price of freedom. God could have made us so that we never sin, but we would not be persons. With all our failures, we represent the highest level of creation, from matter to life, to mind, to spirit. Intrinsic within personhood is the element of choice. All our life is choosing . . . hour after hour, day after day. It is inevitable that if people are free to choose, they are free to make evil choices, choices that can kill thousands of innocent people. We can ask ourselves, which kind of world we would rather have, a world in which all is determined, or a world of freedom, pain, anger, injustice and sin?

5. If God is, and if God is like Christ, as Christians believe, then God is wounded by our pain and sorrow and suffering. Since justice is not done in this life, and we believe in a good, loving and just God, there must be another life in which justice is done. If not, God is defeated. If this life is all, then God's redemptive purpose is defeated.

As a Quaker, I have been taught my entire life to recognize that there is and always will be pain and suffering in the world, and one of my main purposes in this life is to alleviate this pain and suffering as best I can. I have also been taught that pain and suffering is not the end of the story. I was a young boy when I read about a vision that George Fox experienced. It was a vision that has helped me to always place my faith on the positive, centered in the Light. This vision does not deny the problem of suffering and evil, but it points us to the Light where, I believe, our emphasis should be. Fox wrote: "I saw also that there was an ocean of darkness and death, but an infinite ocean of light and love, which flowed over the ocean of darkness." It is in this "ocean of light and love" that I place my faith and my hope.

Has pain and suffering been crippling to your faith?

Have you been able to reconcile a God of love with the issues of suffering and evil?

14.

The Sacrament of Memory

When we are in the midst of our daily lives,
we often miss the hand of God painting the
landscape. We fail to see the mystical way
our lives unfold until later, when we have
time to reflect and to remember . . .

MY MOTHER DIED OF complications due to Alzheimer's disease. When I visited her toward the end of her life, she did not know me. When I talked to her, she did not understand. She sat quietly in the chair by her bed, staring at the floor. Periodically her hands moved, as though she were knitting or playing the piano, both of which she once had done with great skill. As the disease progressed, she became lost in a world that only she knew.

What are we without our memories? What are we without the ability to recall events and places in our lives that have made us who we are? The tragedy of Alzheimer's is the tragedy of lost meaning. To *remember* makes us whole. In the process of *remembering*, we come to understand *who* we are and for *what* purpose we are here. Dementia *dismembers*, leaving the outer peel of our physical existence, while chipping away at the inner core that makes us human.

I am grateful to still possess the ability to remember. More and more I have learned to appreciate remembering as a sacrament and as a vital part of my growth in spirit. My friend Karla Minear, who was my associate when I was the Editor of *Quaker Life* magazine, has written, "Because life is as full of tragedies as it is of joy and love, our memories will be bittersweet. But there is meaning in each bump and rough spot, each bend in the road. Only when we look back can we see the pattern of sunlight and shadow. When we are in the midst of our daily lives, we often miss the hand of God painting the landscape. We fail to see the mystical way our lives unfold until later, when we have time to reflect and to remember."

The tragedy of my mother's situation was that as she aged, she had more time for reflection and remembering, but had lost that ability. I am still learning lessons from my mother, and so at a younger age I have made time to remember and to reflect. This process has taken me in some interesting directions, including a visit to my home community of Muncie, Indiana. While I was growing up there, daily life kept me too busy to express gratitude for Muncie, as well as for my mother. Only recently have I come to fully appreciate my childhood experiences and the lessons they taught.

To help rekindle my memories of Muncie, my mother, and my neighborhood while growing up, I walked the streets and strolled the alleyways. Here I rode my bicycle and drove my '56 Chevy. I stood in front of the place from where I graduated high school and drove by the place that used to be the *Dairy Queen* where I spent many a weekend night "hanging out." Robert Fulghum wrote, "There are places we all come from, deep, rooty, common places, that make us who we are. And we disdain them or treat them lightly at our peril. We turn our back on them at the risk of self-contempt. There is a sense in which we need to go home again and can go home again. Not to recover home, no. But to *sanctify memory*."

Muncie is one of those "deep, rooty, common places" that makes me who I am. As Robert Lynd noted in his book,

Middletown, a sociological study about Muncie, it is a "sober, hopeful, well-meaning city, caught between past and future, and not knowing which way to move." Muncie is a perfect example of a city that is experiencing all the traumas of mid-life, "caught between past and future, and not knowing which way to move."

When I left Muncie for college in Kansas in the summer of 1967, Robert Kennedy and Martin Luther King Jr. were still alive. The Watergate was just an apartment building along the Potomac River in Washington, DC, and most still referred to African Americans as "colored people." Mother Teresa had not yet become an international figure, and the terrorist attack on the World Trade Center in New York City was thirty-four years in the future. My years in Muncie were the years that most Americans still thought that we could win the War in Vietnam, and the most important "social action" on a young man's mind was which party to attend on Friday or Saturday night.

Reflecting on those years from the perspective of the twenty-first century, I find it difficult to believe how tranquil and unassuming the times were. Opioids and other drugs had not become a nationally recognized social problem. AIDS were women in green uniforms who helped nurses in hospitals, and the evening news was only fifteen minutes long. That was a fun and innocent time, not yet marred by the realities of life across town in the racially explosive Whitely section of Muncie, or by the war in southeast Asia.

There is an old neighborhood and home community within each of us. Many of our memories will be bittersweet. That old neighborhood formed us, and we helped to form that neighborhood. We know that time does not stand still, and that changes to our home communities are inevitable. The trees are bigger, the streets narrower, and the houses are smaller and need repair. And the people have all aged, moved away, or now sit in rest homes unable to remember. But those of us who do remember can still claim our roots, paying homage to our experiences, *sanctifying memory.*

"Caught between past and future," writes Robert Lynd of Muncie. A good description of mid-life, but also descriptive of my mother's condition toward the end of her earthly existence. For years she survived physically, confined to the hellish limbo of passing moments. She could not sanctify her own memory, but when I sat with her, she helped me sanctify mine. In the stillness of her room, I studied her face, her hands, her eyes, and I would remember. My heart reached out to her, and I loved. I loved her unconditionally as I remembered the unconditional love this small Quaker woman gave me. She could not remember the physical place, the old neighborhood in which she so proudly and meaningfully reared her family. No, that ability had been taken away from her. But as I looked at her, I felt that she was involved in a much greater spiritual task as she prepared to leave this physical world and enter the world of spirit. In the meantime, she waited, and her son loved, remembered and waited with her.

Allow your memory to take you back to your old neighborhood and the community in which you grew up. What was your family like? Who raised you?

As you reflect on the events in your life, what makes you smile? What makes you cry?

15.

The Sacredness of Chaos

I say to you: one must have chaos in oneself
in order to give birth to a dancing star.

IF WE LIVE LONG enough, we will pass through many life transitions or passages. And if we are sensitive to the stirrings of God within these times of passage, they can become spiritually transforming. Such passages include, the death of a loved one, the wedding of a child, divorce, change of job, position or geographical location, and even the gentle inner tugs on one's soul that acknowledge that the life we are now living is not spiritually fulfilling. All have the potential to lead us into spiritual transformation.

Some of the issues surrounding such transition are *Love and Intimacy*: What are these to me? How do I experience them? *Spirituality and Religion*: Is my religious tradition meeting my spiritual needs? *Work and Family*: How has my work and career defined who I am? How have my work and career intruded into my spiritual and family life? *Relationship and Aloneness*: How do I balance my need for both? *Thinking and Feeling*: How do I make the journey from my head to my heart or, how do I balance my feelings with my thinking? *Freedom and Responsibility*: How do I remain free and independent, and yet responsible for my actions in family and work? *Spouses and Children*: Who am I when I no longer have a spouse or when children no longer "need" me? *Restlessness and Contentment*: How do I handle my feelings of spiritual and emotional restlessness? Where do I experience contentment? *Loss and Death*: How do I face and respond to the death of loved ones? How do I face my own mortality?

These and many other concerns are a part of processing the chaos we feel as we move from one emotional and spiritual place to another. These are sacred concerns. According to the mythology of Genesis, we were created out of chaos, and it is out of chaos, transition, and various life passages that we are re-created anew. It was German philosopher Friedrich Nietzsche who declared, "One must have chaos in oneself in order to give birth to a dancing star." This has certainly been my experience.

One of the major delusions that humans tend to believe is that we have life under control. Diseases can be cured. Sensible precautions and wise laws safeguard us against tragedy. Bridge inspections can keep bridges from collapsing. We can predict economic shifts. We believe that we are intelligent enough to handle anything and everything.

But then those moments in life come where we catch a glimpse of just how fragile we are. Those moments of vulnerability when we hear of another mass shooting, or when planes purposely fly into tall buildings, or the earth shakes, or when we experience disease and heartbreak. These moments confront us with the stark and terrifying reality that, despite our advanced technology and five-year plans, we are not as in control as we thought. These are moments of reality, when we recognize that our worldly power and money, our many connections, or whatever else we may have that keeps us in control, *cannot save us*. In these vulnerable moments we realize that living in North America, complete with border walls or immigration policies designed to keep the "riff raff" of the world on the outside, cannot insulate us from what is happening in other parts of the world, or the economic forces of unemployment and a changing job market, or the tragedy of too many guns in the hands of too many unstable people, or terminal illness, divorce, or death.

In the vulnerability of chaos, we become ever-more conscious of the greatest of human adventures, *spiritual growth*. In the end, we are spiritual beings in search of connection with the Inner Light, i.e. the Living God. Chaos intensifies this quest. Whatever else we thought the meaning of life to be before we experienced chaos, we now know that that meaning has changed. In chaos we learn that life is a shifting fault line, and that there is no such thing as a solid foundation.

Within the tragedies that we experience, either personally or within community, country, and world, a space will open within us, and in that vulnerability, the Inner Light shines most brightly. This is where the sacred and chaos meet, and where warp speed spiritual growth takes place.

How have you experienced chaos in your life?

Has such chaos helped you to grow spiritually?

16.

Twilight of the Soul

Why are you cast down, O my soul,
and why are you disquieted within me?

FEW COULD IMAGINE MY relief and gratitude when I saw the sun rise last week. It was a brief respite from the gloomy and overcast days of winter in the Ohio Valley. However, the dark days have been fitting, since I have been going through a rather gloomy time myself; feeling that God was distant and that I was just going through the motions of living. It was not a full-blown "dark night of the soul," but rather a *twilight of the soul.* I have been through these periods at other times in my life, and so I know they will eventually pass. Perhaps the weather was the trigger for this darkness, or what is happening in Washington, DC. Maybe the report of another school shooting brings me low. Perhaps it is just the "winter blues," whatever that is supposed to be. I don't know. I do know that when these feelings of spiritual dryness come over me, the creative process by which I live, tends to slow down.

During twilight times of dryness, how does one remain hopeful and continue to grow spiritually? Just "wait it out?" Are there some pro-active steps that can help me move beyond these feelings? I believe that there are.

To maintain faith and hope during these difficult times, I find help in establishing a more *disciplined routine*. Discipline has always been an important part of my spiritual growth, but in times of dryness I need it more than ever. To discipline myself to meditate daily and to read various spiritual writings is helpful. Regular times of physical exercise lift my spirits when I am feeling "cast down." With Richard Foster, the Quaker author of *Celebration of Discipline*, I know that any growth involves discipline.

Another way to maintain hope and faith during times of *twilight*, is to *connect with others*. Anyone experiencing a dark night or twilight of the soul almost naturally withdraws into him or herself. As with so many other aspects of spiritual growth, connecting with others in community, where sorrows are divided and where I am assured of love and encouragement, is a good way to combat spiritual dryness.

Hope and faith are also emboldened by intentional efforts to *serve others*. Again, focusing inward is natural during difficult times. Serving others puts our problems in perspective. Volunteering at a social service agency or hospital or holding the hand of a frightened child, or distraught family who does not know where homelessness will take them tonight, will lighten the burden of the depression.

My favorite Psalm is number forty-two. "As a hart longs for flowing streams," the psalmist writes, "so longs my soul for thee, O God. My soul thirsts for God, for the living God." There have been times in my life when I understand the psalmist's "longing soul and thirst for God." I know about "disquieted feelings" and the sense of being "cast down."

But I also know about hope. I know that what I am feeling now is temporary. In the end, and in the core of my being, I can say with the psalmist, "Hope in God, for I shall again praise him, my help and my God."

*Have you experienced times of spiritual dryness
and longing for God?*

*During such times, in what ways have you found the hope
needed to sustain your faith?*

Part IV.

PATH OF A SEEKER

17.

Seeking Discernment

How can I make the best choices
for a God-Centered, meaningful life?

"WHY?" HAS BEEN A refrain throughout my life. "But how?" and "What if?" have filled the spaces in between. I love questions. Despite the inherent expectation of an answer in each question, I have often found that in the tension between the asking of the question and the answer there is the greatest possibility for understanding. As in most profound educational and spiritual adventures, wisdom does not come in the answer, whatever it may be, but in asking the question.

To get at the heart of understanding God and how God wants me to live, asking questions is central. At the root, to question is to be on a *quest*. Whether we recognize it or not, we are all on a journey to discern who God is, why we are here, and how we can live so that we have not only life but have a life that is *meaningful*. In his book, *The Sacred Journey*, the prolific writer, Frederick Buechner shares how each of our various experiences of *journey* are centered in *search*. "We search for a self to be. We search for other selves to love. We search for work to do. And since even when to one degree or another we find these things, we find also that there is still something crucial missing which we have not found, we search for that unfound thing too, even though we do not know its name or where it is to be found or even if it is to be found at all." My search for what Buechner calls "that unfound thing" is guided through the asking of queries.

1. Is Love and Care a part of the choice I am making?

I have a close friend who was a counseling psychologist at a veterans' home, where he led a weekly support group. One man was near total incapacitation, but nonetheless, attended this group. He moved around in a wheelchair, pushing himself backward with his only leg, refusing help from anyone. Because of his injuries, his body leaned to one side, and his head rested sideways on his shoulder. He was a faithful member of the group, even though it took him an hour to get ready and wheel himself from his room to the meeting place. He never spoke, *until one day.*

A fellow veteran was lamenting that his life had no meaning. He had thought that life could have meaning by helping others, but now he felt that meaning had been taken away. Having been put away until death in one of society's "holding cells," he was the one needing help. The veteran in the wheelchair listened intently to the other man's lament, echoed by others in the group. As the session ended, the silent, one-legged man turned to his fellow veteran who had led the "life has no meaning" discussion, and spoke for the first time, asking, "Will you help me back to my room?"

Meaning in life can be found in the many great and small acts of love and care that we do for one another.

2. Is the choice I am making one where Truth and Integrity are present?

Truth and integrity are at the core of who I am as a person, and who I believe God is as Spirit. *Truth* and *Integrity* have been very important to Quakers throughout their history, so important that *Integrity* is one of our testimonies. If I make a choice where my integrity is compromised and where truth is absent, I can assume that such a choice or choices are not a part of a God-centered, meaningful life.

3. Is the choice I am making one that promotes the cause of Justice and Righteousness in the world?

God's first requirement as expressed in Micah 6:8 is "to do justice." I believe that God is a God of justice, and that we are called to expose injustice and work for justice whenever and wherever we can. The prophet Amos declared, "let justice roll down like waters, and righteousness like an ever-flowing stream." (5:24) A meaningful life involves choices that lead to acts of justice and righteousness for all people.

4. Is the choice I am making one where Beauty and a sense of Awe find expression?

God is present in all that lifts my spirit into a sense of awe. Life experiences that put our souls in a place where we know true spiritual beauty, whether it is found in persons or in nature, is to connect with the Living God. In the sense of awe that results, I feel connected to the Inner Light of God and experience a more meaningful life.

The quest for a meaningful life will involve, *Love and Care, Truth and Integrity, Justice and Righteousness, Beauty and a sense of Awe.* All are universal values that can be incorporated into every person's unique search for meaning.

Are there other queries that would be helpful in the quest for a meaningful, God-Centered life?

How can you make reflective discernment a part of your daily life?

18.

Recovering Passion

I am on a quest to recover passion.

As I get older, I find myself focusing more and more on those things that give my life passion. I am also becoming aware of those things that take my passion away. I have a friend who talks about the 80/20 rule of life. We know that some life experiences will drain and de-energize us. He contends that around 20 percent of life is "grunt" work that de-energizes our spirits. If we can have passion for 80 percent of our experiences, we will remain spiritually and emotionally healthy. When the ratio becomes 70/30 or 60/40, then we can get into trouble with our emotions and spirit. There have been times when I have felt my passion for life waning and dipping into a place that is not healthy, and there have been times when I was so filled with passion for what I was doing that it could barely be contained. When my passion for life waned, I have heeded the signs, and set my life on a spiritual journey of seeking more of what is missing.

Passion can be an elusive word, much like spirituality. This said, I can try and work out some rather broad definitive parameters:

Our English term *passion* comes from the Latin "passio," which can be defined as "overwhelming emotion." Such emotion will be experienced in many ways throughout life, whether in sorrow or suffering or happiness and joy. In all ways passion will carry within it the element of *intensity*, whether this intensity is an experience of great sorrow or great joy. Some will experience passion as the fuel that ignites a search for a more meaningful existence, or as the stimulus to drive toward an ideal. Most of us will recognize when we are experiencing passion in our lives, and we will most certainly recognize its absence.

Many things can cause the loss of passion and intensity in life. Here are four:

First, *passion is the price paid for worldly security.* A life constantly seeking a larger savings account or a better pension plan, will pay with spiritual passion. As the desire for security becomes stronger, we usually take fewer and fewer risks, and we settle into a comfortable pattern where the fuel of passion is replaced by secure boredom. Each of us will have to determine how much worldly security we need, and how much passion we are willing to pay for it. I have found that in paying too much, true meaning in life and the passion surrounding such meaning can be lost.

Secondly, *the loss of passion is the result of living a life of dichotomy* or living out someone else's story. Whenever we live out someone else's expectations of how we should be living, or when we mask ourselves and hide the reality of who we truly are, we pay with a loss of passion.

During a seminar I led on spiritual autobiography, one of the participants remarked to me, "I've just realized that I've been living out my father's story rather than my own story!" One step in passion recovery begins with recognizing that many of us have been living lives of dichotomy, trying to be the self that others want us to be, rather than being our real selves.

Sam Keen is a mythologist who led seminars on storytelling. Using the language of the computer age, he talked about how each of us is equipped at birth with "hard drives." As we mature, we are constantly being given "software," the stories of family, the stories of culture, the stories of our religion, until we find ourselves living out all the stories that others have given us. Keen's point was that our mental and spiritual health requires us to discover our *own* story and learn what is separating us from that story. This does not mean rejecting all the stories we are given in this life. That would be an impossible task to undertake even if we tried. It does mean, however, that we must become conscious of what has been given to us, rather than *unconsciously* living out others' expectations. In the words of Howard Thurman, "follow the grain in your own wood."

Third, *the loss of passion is closely associated with the fears that govern our lives.* Fear can control our lives: the fear of rejection, the fear of economic failure, the fear of vulnerability, the fear of death and dying, the fear of being seen and understood for who we truly are rather than the false selves we have anxiously projected. Our fears keep us from experiencing life in all its abundance, leaving us trapped within a cell of our own making, and going through the motions of living, but not living *fully.*

Finally, *a loss of passion occurs where there is no outlet.* One of the best ways I have learned to recover passion in my life is to focus outside of myself, and to work for good beyond my own selfish desires. Many years ago, someone shared an illustration of this point that I have never forgotten. The difference between the Sea of Galilee and the Dead Sea is that the Sea of Galilee has an outlet, the Jordan River. This is what keeps the Galilean Sea vibrant and alive. Without an outlet we too become dead.

One of my best friends, Captain Larry Walker, who was the President of World-Wide Marine Training in Oriental, North Carolina, told me shortly before his death that he was on *a quest to recover passion.* And aren't we all? Such a quest is a spiritual quest, one in which God walks and runs with us. We are finite spiritual beings in search of a connection with the passionate, life- giving love of the Infinite Living God or Inner Light. I believe this is a *universal* truth. Each of us is also a *unique* story which is constantly unfolding as the search progresses. I have been helped in my search when I pay attention to the ways I can renew passion in my life, by being aware of how much I am paying with passion for worldly security, by seeking to become real and to live out my own story, by walking through the paper walls of the fears that keep me bound and separated from God's surrounding love, and by becoming involved in outlets of caring and loving service.

*What have been the circumstances in your life
when you have lost a sense of passion?*

What has been helpful to you in the recovery of passion?

19.

Risking Vulnerability

To grow up is to accept vulnerability . . .
To be alive is to be vulnerable.

RECENTLY MY HIGH SCHOOL class celebrated its fiftieth graduation anniversary in Muncie, Indiana. I am a graduate of Burris Laboratory School, located on the campus of Ball State University. Our reunion was filled with many stories of remembrance and lots of laughter. For me, high school was a time of learning to be a social being. Yes, that it was about history and Latin and geometry, to be sure, but my social life always came first on my priority list.

As a teenager growing up in Muncie, my search for meaning in life was played out through the lyrical creativity of the Beatles' hits, "I Want to Hold Your Hand," and "I Saw Her Standing There." Friday and Saturday nights found me with a group of friends, either looking for a party where girls were, or finding a party with girls, and then acting as though their presence didn't matter. At these parties, most of the boys gathered in a corner of the room and talked about one of two things: basketball or fast cars. The scent of colognes with names like, Jade East, English Leather, and British Sterling filled the air, and phrases like Pontiac GTO, Oldsmobile

442, and Oscar Robertson flowed in endless succession. Such were the main topics of conversation in 1960s Indiana, especially for boys. The only deviation from this pattern was when the month of May rolled around, and that month the Indy 500 was our focus. The dance floor loomed large at the center of these parties. As a somewhat shy teen, I went to many of these events before I attempted to dance. The first time I did dance, or *tried* to dance, I made sure the dance was a slow one. I had not yet mastered the intricacies of fast movement with another human being. And so, when it was time, I mustered all the courage I could, walked to the other side of the room, and asked this cute girl to dance. She accepted and we began. Although I felt clumsy and awkward at first, I quickly gained confidence in what I believed to be "smooth moves" and "magic" on the dance floor. Everything was right, my hand on hers, and our cheeks touching. We were a couple!

Into this scene of tranquil bliss, the unthinkable happened. Although it occurred in a flash, the memory is still as vivid for me now as it was at the age of fifteen. My right foot leapt from the floor and planted itself into the shin of my unsuspecting partner. I remember this cute girl yelping like a wounded animal, grabbing her shin, and suggesting that we not continue. In shocked confusion, I stood alone on the darkened dance floor, while "Smoke Gets in Your Eyes" by the Platters softly faded into the background. I watched in horror as my partner, former partner, limped to a chair on the side of the room, and a group of girls gathered around consoling her. I felt naked and vulnerable, as if the whole world was watching me make a fool of myself. In fact, *my* whole world, the world that mattered to me, *was* watching. Making my way back to the group of guys in the corner, the group that was talking fast cars and basketball when I had made my courageous walk to the dance floor, I was stricken to learn that my dancing ability was the *new* topic of conversation; "Hey, Newby, looking good out there." "You really won her heart." "What are you going to do next, hit her in the mouth!" A long time and many hours of dance practice alone in my room passed before I again attempted the art of dancing.

The unspoken rule in adolescence is to keep quiet about weaknesses out of fear of ridicule by peers. The last thing that anyone wants at that age, or any age for that matter, is to become the subject of jokes and teasing. And so, we stumble through difficult times alone, in search of maturity and most protective of the thin veneer of *coolness* which, we believe, must be protected at all costs. Over the years, we learn what to expose about ourselves and what to keep hidden. As a result, we grow up skilled at hiding, and closed to new possibilities where we might be hurt.

Vulnerability. It is a word that takes on more and more spiritual meaning as we mature. Experiencing change, and moving from one chapter of life to another, we will confront *new ways* that challenge our *old ways* and well-ordered patterns of living. As uncomfortable as leaving one pattern of life for another can be, such change and movement in life is also a way we become closer to the Inner Light of God, a God who is continuously taking risks and becoming vulnerable in staying connected to us. In our vulnerable discomfort, God opens our hearts and challenges us to explore new possibilities. The more open and vulnerable we become, the more authentic we can be with others, the closer we will feel to the Living God, and the more intimate will be our relationships. The author, Madeleine L' Engle, has written, "When we were children, we used to think that when we grew-up we would no longer be vulnerable. But to grow-up is to accept vulnerability. To be alive is to be vulnerable."

At my fiftieth-class reunion, I saw my one-time dance partner, now a mature and dignified woman. I took a deep breath, garnered my courage, and strolled over to talk to her about that memorable dance. Do you know what? She could not even remember it! What had haunted me for fifty-three years, wasn't even a blip on her memory screen. One of my first major experiences of courage was not remembered by the primary object of my bravery. Arriving home, I reflected on my reunion experiences, and I decided to become vulnerable again. I invited my fifteen-year-old dance partner to be one of my "Friends" on Facebook. Over three weeks have passed, and still no response.

I guess the inner issues around vulnerability, embarrassment, hurt, shame, etc., take a lifetime to process. The good news is that I am not alone in this inner work; the vulnerable, Living God continues to work with me.

In what ways have you made yourself vulnerable?

How have you grown spiritually
through risking vulnerability?

20.

Queries and Spiritual Growth

... what shapes our lives are questions we ask,
refuse to ask, or never think of asking.

ASKING QUESTIONS TO AID in spiritual nurture has long been a practice within the Quaker faith. Being a non-creedal tradition, queries or questions have been the medium through which the Society of Friends has kept alive their testimonies of *peace, simplicity, integrity, community, equality and stewardship of the earth.*

Again, the author Sam Keen has been helpful in writing about questions and the human spirit in *Spirituality and Health* Magazine, saying, "What you ask is who you are," and "What shapes our lives are questions we ask, refuse to ask, or never think of asking." Two queries are constant companions in my life:

1. What outward things and inner attitudes separate me from a closer relationship to God?

Many outward distractions in my life disrupt my relationship to God. I am grateful to Quaker author Richard Foster for his exploration of *Fasting* in the modern world, enlarging the definition beyond merely foregoing food, to rejecting anything that gets in the way of connecting with the Light of God. Loud music, cable news, the cell phone, etc., can all disrupt my spiritual life.

Not only outward things can separate me from God, but inner attitudes can as well. Earlier in this volume I wrote about *simmering*. Queries can lead us into times of *simmering* when we reflect on our inner attitudes and how they affect our relationship with God. For example, I know that I can have a critical spirit. For much of my life, I lived in the world of academia, which is built upon the Socratic method of asking questions. Such a methodology leads to critical thought. The trick is to use this method at the right times, and not allow it to interfere in relationships with others. The word, "idiot" can slip out too easily when I am listening to someone else speak, especially if that person is an elected official. The other day I was watching an interview with a congressman from Ohio. The interview was not a dialogue between reporter and congressman, but a monologue. Trite phrases and misconstrued thoughts spewed from the congressman's mouth. He showed no evidence of being able to stop and think, or to reflect upon anything that the reporter was asking. All he could do was talk fast and share clichés.

And yet the congressman is a child of God and the word, "idiot" does not help build God's kingdom on Earth. Critical thinking is an important tool in seeking truth. Personal criticism that leads to judging others can damage our souls.

The world can be a negative place where we hurt others and where we can be hurt, either by words or by actions. By pondering the query, "What are the outward things and inner attitudes that separate me from a closer relationship to God?" I become aware of those things that interfere with my relationships with others and with my God.

> 2. Do I manifest a forgiving spirit and care for the reputation of others?

The second query gets to the heart of where I need to grow spiritually. President Kennedy was once asked if he forgave his enemies. His response, "Of course I forgive my enemies, but I never forget their names!" President Kennedy is to be commended for his willingness to forgive, but our spiritual growth depends on forgetting as well. It is so easy to carry grudges and feel animosity toward those who have harmed us, or whom we perceive have harmed us. To paraphrase Nelson Mandela, anti-apartheid activist and first black president of South Africa, as he was leaving prison, *I knew that I would never be totally free if I did not leave my hatred behind me in the prison I left.* By not forgiving others, we imprison ourselves.

To care for the reputation of others means to refuse to participate in gossip or to pass along hurtful allegations that are mean-spirited and based on half-truths. Again, it is so easy to delight in the failings of others, that we believe will make us appear more righteous.

A few years ago, I was planning a conference and wanted to include a soloist as part of the program. I called Rebecca, who was a part of a congregation in the South, and with whom I had become acquainted during a trip to England. Rebecca was a devout Christian with a beautiful voice. When I asked her to participate in the conference, she responded, "Jim, do you know what has been going on down here?" I responded that I did not. She began to cry as she shared her story of sexual involvement with her married pastor. "He has resigned, divorced, and moved away. I am still here, but I can't go anywhere for the shame and embarrassment. I have lost my job as the church soloist and none of my friends will talk to me. I feel so guilty and ashamed."

Listening to the full extent of her pain reminded me of the words of a colleague who declared, "Christians shoot their own wounded." This may be an overstatement, but there is truth in this observation as well.

Forgiveness is central to both Judaism and Christianity. Most notable within the Jewish tradition is the "Year of Jubilee," when debts are forgiven, and former debtors are given an opportunity to begin anew. Within the Christian tradition is the response of Jesus to Peter's question, "How many times Lord, must I forgive. Till seven times?" Jesus' responded, "Not seven times, but seventy times seven." (Matthew 18:22) In other words, forgiveness is to become a part of who we are. No one can forgive that many times without forgiveness becoming a basic tenet in his or her life. And yet, how hard it is to forgive. To harbor a grudge, to scapegoat others, to hurt another to raise one's own status in the world, or to just wound another's heart, is to cause pain to our own souls. To learn forgiveness is difficult soul work but it is essential to spiritual growth.

*What are those outward things and inner attitudes
in your life that are separating you from a
closer relationship to God?*

*Who are the Rebeccas in your life who await a healing
touch, a kind and encouraging word, a forgiving spirit?*

21.

A Life of Paradox

Spiritual growth is the process by which we seek
to know and be known by the Living God.
This can follow many paths, but it will
inevitably lead us into the world of paradox.

MY QUAKER FAITH HAS taught me the value of quiet, reflective thought, and that has led me into the world of paradox. A careful reading of scripture shows how much the Christian faith is a faith of paradox. The Kingdom of God, Jesus tells us, is great, and yet compares it to a tiny mustard seed. In such a Kingdom the poor are blessed, the first are last, the weak are made strong, whoever exalts himself will be humbled, and whoever humbles himself will be exalted. Paradox!

As I have traveled my path of spiritual growth, five major paradoxes have emerged, which have helped clarify the complexities of human nature and the world in which we live.

The first paradox is *the paradox of spiritual growth*, or the more I grow spiritually, the further from spiritual perfection I will realize I am. On this important point of humility, all the spiritual evidence of the ages agrees. A leading indicator of this truth is found in countless passages of scripture and the classics of devotion, including these words from William Law, the eighteenth century Anglican priest: "We may as well think to see without eyes or live without breath, as to live in the spirit of religion without the spirit of humility."

A second paradox, closely related to the first, can be called *the paradox of spiritual enlightenment,* or the more enlightened I become as an adult, the more child-like my wisdom will be. Jesus said that we must become like children to enter the Kingdom of God, and Ben Hoff has written in the *Tao of Pooh* that, "An adult is not the highest stage of development. The end cycle is that of the independent, clear-minded, all seeing child that is the level known as wisdom. Why do the enlightened seem filled with light and happiness like children? Why do they sometimes look and even talk like children? Because they are."

Children delight in mystery and follow their hearts. Children know that there is a lot to know and discover, and that the more they learn and discover, there is still more to learn and discover. Children are perpetual questioners and love the process of seeking.

A third paradox may be called *the paradox of knowing and mystery,* or, if I am to know God, I must be comfortable in mystery. I have written about being comfortable in mystery in previous chapters. Suffice to say, no matter how much we seek to define God and "systematize" our process of knowing, there will always be mystery beyond our knowledge. Again, author Madeline L' Engle has written, "We need to fall on our knees in front of the mystery." In the tension we experience between affirming our faith in one breath and asking questions about our life and faith in the next, is to accept our human frailty. The more we come to know God, the more there will be to discover.

A fourth paradox is *the paradox of separation and connection,* or the more detached from this world I become, the more intensely I am connected to it. If we are growing spiritually, the familiar attachments to this world will begin to loosen, and our hearts will fill with compassion for others. In the words of professor and author China Galland, "To have the heart of the world inside of you means you will feel another's suffering inside your own body, and you will weep." The new computer, cell phone, or fast car that once promised to fill the void in our lives no longer does. We find that we are becoming more concerned with the well-being of others. We lose our taste for self-righteousness and judgmentalism and become accepting and loving in new ways.

Mother Teresa was asked why she bothered taking care of the street people of Calcutta, knowing that they will die within a few hours. To those who do not understand this paradox of separation and connection, she is wasting her time. Her response: "Because I want them to know, if even for a few minutes, that there was someone in this world who loved them." For Mother Teresa, the material lures of this world were not important, but the world's poor, starving and sick *were* important, and became her world of ministry. She was a living model of what is meant by separation from this world, but deeply connected in a *new* way.

A fifth and final paradox for me is *the paradox of love,* or the more love I want to experience, the more love I must give away. If there is a universal truth that we know experientially, it is that we want to be loved. We are told that God is love. And yet love can only be ours if we give it to others. The more we give, the greater the return. Trying to control or possess love is like trying to hold a sunbeam. It cannot be done. Love will, however, come back to us, when we give it away.

Through reflective thought, my Quaker faith has helped me understand the importance of paradox in my life of spiritual growth. And true to the definition of paradox, the more I understand it, the more I find there is to understand. Such is the cycle of spiritual learning.

Is paradox a part of your spiritual growth?

*How has paradox helped you make sense
of the world and your faith?*

22.

Life Lessons

I expect to pass through this world but once . . .

I HAVE BEEN THINKING a lot lately about life and the lessons gleaned from my experiences. Perhaps it is because I have just learned about the death of a friend, or because I spent most of the fall dealing with my sister's serious health problems. From September to January, she was in the hospital and rehabilitation, not expected to live. The good news is that she is now home and watching more basketball than any other living being! I have been forced to consider the *lesson of mortality*. It is a lesson that teaches us that our physical life on this earth will come to an end. Reflecting on this lesson, I think of the words attributed to the French Quaker, Stephen Grellet: "I expect to pass through this world but once. Any kindness that I can show, or any burden that I can lift, let me do it now, let me not withhold or defer it, for I shall not pass this way again."

This physical world is one aspect of the continuum of life. I have faith that there is a spiritual world where we continue to grow in love. The *lesson of mortality* is the truth that no one gets out of this world physically alive. But the *lessons of immortality* and *faith* teach that we will continue to live in the world of spirit.

In Elaine Pagels' book, *Why Religion?* she shares her life story intermixed with her study of the gospel of Thomas. Her work on the gospel of Thomas and the Jesus sayings therein, helped Pagels emerge from the grief and darkness she felt after the deaths of her young son and husband. She wrote, "A primary theme within the Jewish mystical tradition is that the image of God and divine light given in creation, is hidden deep within each of us, linking our fragile, limited selves to their divine source." Even if we are unaware of this Inner Light, the Thomas sayings urge us to keep seeking until we find it. Thomas wrote, "Within a person of light, there is light. If illuminated, it lights up the whole world, if not, everything is dark." Such revelations helped Elaine Pagels dispel her feelings of isolation and turn her from despair to hope. She felt a mystical connection with lost loved ones and felt a part of that mysterious fabric of the universe connecting all people with each other and with God. Reading *Why Religion?* helped me understand why Elaine Pagels feels such an affinity with the Quakers.

A second lesson that continues to crop up in my times of reflection is closely associated with the first. It is *the lesson of change and evolution.* I will expand on this lesson in chapter 27. It is the recognition that everything in this world is in a constant state of flux. Everything is always changing. Just when we think we can count on the constancy of something, it changes.

In my book, *Sacred Chaos,* I write about wanting to hold on to an awakening spiritual experience and protect it from change. I liken that experience to walking on the beach with God and finding a beautiful sand dollar. I stop and build a sandcastle around the shell, hoping to protect it. Soon, however, waves are lapping at the protective wall, and I cannot hold back the tide. Looking up, I discover that God is walking ahead and had not stopped. I start to walk again but continue to strain my neck, looking back at the sand dollar. Finally, the sand dollar is out of sight, and I look forward to the possibility of new sand dollar discoveries.

Because of our comfort with things as they are, we want to hold on to the past. Change and movement, however, are inevitable. The good news is that there are new spiritual discoveries in our present and future. We will always have memory of the past, but if we are to continue to grow spiritually, we need to be open to new spiritual discoveries. Such is the life lesson of change and movement.

A third lesson of life that I have recently been contemplating is the *importance of friendships*. As I have been working through the lessons of mortality and change and evolution, I have recognized anew the value of friendships, and the truth that we need one another to help us through the important lessons of life. Friendships worth anything are energizing and sustaining. The lesson of friendship is that however many miles separate us or however many months have passed since we have seen one another, sustaining and enduring friendships can be a part of our lives throughout our time on Earth.

During a very difficult time I became good friends with a former Roman Catholic priest James Kavanaugh, who left the priesthood to become a poet and counselor. Jim called me and I would call him whenever we wanted to share something important, or just have a listening ear when either of us was feeling low. I knew Jim through his books long before I ever met him in person. His book, *There Are Men Too Gentle to Live Among Wolves*, was particularly helpful to me during a time of depression and spiritual chaos. Another of his books, however, *Will You Be My Friend*, has been of lasting influence and I continue to refer to it today. Jim left this earthly life in 2009, but he continues to live in his writings. In *Will You Be My Friend*, he wrote:

Will you be my friend? There are so many reasons why you never should:
I'm sometimes sullen, often shy, acutely sensitive, my fear erupts as anger.
I find it hard to give, I talk about myself when I'm afraid
and often spend a day without anything to say.
But I will make you laugh and love you quite a bit
and hold you when you're sad.
I cry a little almost every day because I'm more caring than the strangers
ever know,
and if at times, I show my tender side (the soft and warmer part I hide)

I wonder, will you be my friend?
A friend who far beyond the feebleness of any vow or tie
will touch the secret place where I am really I,
to know the pain of lips that plead and eyes that weep,
who will not run away when you find me in the street
alone and lying mangled by my quota of defeats
but will stop and stay, to tell me of another day
when I was beautiful. Will you be my friend?

Will you be my friend? The question reaches into the heart of what being human means. Who among us does not want someone to make us laugh and love us quite a bit? Over the years I have learned, and continue to learn, the lesson of the importance of friendship.

And then there is *the lesson of patience.* A few years ago, our daughter graduated from Indiana University. She is our only child, so she is a bit spoiled, but very bright. I was never sure, however, until I saw the actual diploma, that she was going to make it through college. As bright as she is, she had a difficult time applying her mind to her schoolwork. When given a choice between a party and studying for an exam, she would always choose the party. As she shared with me one time at the height of her party going years, her favorite sorority on campus was, *Tap-A-Keg-Of-Brew!* I spent many a night filled with anxiety worrying about her. When is she going to get serious about life? Will she ever think of anyone but herself? When, dear God, will her "teachable" or "awakening" moment come?!?

As I have reflected on her high school and college life, I have recognized that my daughter reminds me a lot of myself. If I had a chance to go out with my friends or to a party, the schoolwork would have to wait. It was not until the latter part of my college career that I became serious about my studies and began to have intelligent conversations with my parents. As I proceeded in the academic process, my father would say, "I knew you had it in you." I liked hearing that, and I enjoyed making my parents proud.

Sitting in the rain at the football stadium of Indiana University, I looked down at my daughter, one of thousands graduating, and said to my wife, Elizabeth, "I knew she had it in her." Knowing of my impatience throughout Lisa's growing years and academic life, Elizabeth turned to me with a look that said, "Yeah, right!" I guess that the "I knew she had it in her" was always covered with a few layers of anxiety and impatience.

A friend of mine has a t-shirt that says, "The older I get the wiser I was!" We tend to forget our own foibles, mistakes, and times of impatience. Upon reflection we were always more poised, more patient, more loving, more knowledgeable than was the case. Life is like that. We are our own revisionist historians.

Many life lessons have filled the path of this seeker. The *lesson of mortality*, the *lesson of change and evolution*, the *lesson of friendship*, and the *lesson of patience* are four life lessons that I have learned and continue to learn along life's continuum.

*What are the life lessons that have been
on your mind and heart recently?
How have you changed your life as a result?*

23.

A Light in the Darkness

And then, into this tasteless heap of gold
and marble, He came . . .

RECENTLY I WATCHED A political rally in Ohio, starring President Trump. By anyone's standards of civility, the event was very disconcerting. People were yelling obscenities and lifting their middle fingers at the press. Predictably, there were the "Make America Great Again" hats and t-shirts to be expected at such rallies. But there were also t-shirts with the slogan, "I'd rather be a Russian than a Democrat." All in all, the scene was difficult to watch, and so, after a few minutes, I quit watching.

I think I understand the frustration and anger of the rally attendees. For several years, our nation has gone through a time of distrust, of the press, of the Congress, of banks, and so on. It is not an exaggeration to say that a large swath of our country no longer believes that the institutions that have had as their main purpose to uphold our civilization, are no longer working. At least many feel that they are no longer working for the common person.

A few years ago, writers Ron Fournier and Sophie Quinton, wrote an article for *The Atlantic*, titled, "In Nothing We Trust." This article attracted me because it focused on my hometown Muncie,

Indiana. Sociological studies often refer to Muncie as "Middle-town, USA." Fournier and Quinton interviewed a man who had lost his job. His wife had also lost her job. The bank had foreclosed on their home because the modification the couple had worked out was cancelled, and they could not come up with the eighteen-hundred dollars in back payments. This couple felt betrayed by a society that no longer valued them.

The statistics in this article suggest that the feelings of the couple in Muncie are widespread. Seven in ten Americans believed that the country is on the wrong track. Eight in ten were dissatis-fied with the way the nation was being governed. Only twenty-three percent had confidence in banks, and just nineteen percent had confidence in big business. Less than half of the respondents expressed "a great deal" of confidence in the public-school sys-tem or organized religion. The article quoted sociology professor, Laura Hansen: "We have lost our gods. We have lost faith in the media; we have lost faith in our culture. We have lost that basic sense of trust and confidence in everything." Professor Hansen continued, "When people trust their institutions, they are better able to solve common problems. Research shows that school prin-cipals are much more likely to turn around struggling schools in places where people have a history of working together and get-ting involved in their children's education. Communities bonded by friendships formed at religious institutions are more likely to vote, volunteer, and perform every day good deeds like helping someone find a job. And governments find it easier to persuade the public to make sacrifices for the common good when people trust their political leaders to have the community's best interests at heart."

It may have been over two-thousand years ago, but it was also very much like the time in which we are now living. There was a growing gap between the very rich and the poor. Those under occupied Roman rule lacked trust in traditional institutions, with religious leaders collaborating with the occupying force of Rome. Those in Roman leadership showed a general lack of concern for those persons society considered expendables, the "under the bridge" dwellers of that day. Politicians in Rome argued over matters that rarely helped or affected the general population, and people suspected anyone in authority.

In his novel, *Doctor Zhivago*, Boris Pasternak wrote about Roman culture and the way Jesus changed that culture: "Rome was a flea market of borrowed gods and conquered peoples, a bargain basement on two floors, earth and heaven, a mass of filth convoluted in a triple knot as in an intestinal obstruction. Dacians, Herulians, Scythians, Sarmatians, Hyperboreans, heavy wheels without spokes, illiterate emperors, fish fed on the flesh of learned slaves . . . all crammed into the passages of the Coliseum, and all wretched.

"And then, into this tasteless heap of gold and marble, He came, light and clothed in an aura, emphatically human, deliberately provincial Galilean, and at that moment gods and nations ceased to be and humans came into being . . ."

My path as a seeker has led me to try to understand the times in which we are now living. The angry political rallies, the distrust of institutions, the fear and racism, and so on. In the words of the author and scholar, Marcus Borg, I find myself at a place of seeking to "meet Jesus again for the first time," and understand the radical love that surrounded his life, and how his life might give us hope today. I have many questions: *Who was this man who so upset the Roman Empire that they killed him? Who was this "deliberately provincial Galilean" who lived in such a manner that those who knew him best became convinced that he represented a divine breakthrough in human history? What was so special about Jesus and the way he interacted with others that our understanding of God changed radically? How did his followers experience the light and love within this man that pierced the darkness of the time in which they were living?*

I believe that through the centuries Jesus attracted so many to him because of his understanding that *God is love.* In his book, *Unlearning God*, Quaker author, Philip Gulley has written: "So God is love, right? Well, that depends on how we understand love. I'm reluctant to ascribe human emotions to God, as if God were an extrapolation of humanity. . . I believe that God is that essence in us that reaches out to another, committed to their well being, their enlightenment, their moral, emotional, relational, and spiritual growth." I love this definition of the God of love. Jesus embodied this kind of love in his own life in a radical way that gave his life its richness and ultimate meaning.

Such radical love leads to actions for justice and for the good of humanity that are risky and challenge many of society's norms. If life is lived in love, we will find ourselves questioning the vast sums of money that our government spends on wars, past, present and future. We will begin to question the validity of spending billions of dollars to build a wall between Mexico and the United States, when the cry for it is based on lies, half-truths, and made-up fears. Few expressions are more antithetical to the wall-smashing love of Jesus than, "Build the wall," or "Finish the wall." The radical love displayed by Jesus embraces diversity in all its beauty: diversity in race, class, gender and sexual orientation. The radical love that Jesus demonstrated, beckons us to live better than we are living.

This kind of love does not just happen. People have choices. People can decide that the life that they are living is not as good as it gets, that it can be richer and more spiritually fulfilling. To see and understand life through the lens of radical love means seeing through the myriad of un-loving distractions that are obstructing our sight and limiting us spiritually and emotionally.

History is filled with persons who lived lives based on this love, that has moved them to upset the tables in the temples of their own time. Within my own Quaker tradition, these disrupters include George Fox, Margaret Fell, John Woolman, and Bayard Rustin, to name a few. Within the wider Christian tradition there was Martin Luther King Jr., Dorothy Day, Mother Teresa, and many others. We are drawn to these persons because in their lives there is hope, and in our times, hope is that for which we all yearn. The hope to which we cling is the hope that life can be better.

I recently attended a writer's workshop at Princeton Theological Seminary. Anne Lamott was one of the presenters. In the question and answer period, an audience member asked her, "How do we respond to the current political and social environment in our country?" In essence, her response was, "Go out and feed the hungry, care for the sick, love the unlovable, and give people hope that our better angels will win out in the end."

And into this tasteless heap of gold and marble, He came, light and clothed in an aura, emphatically human, deliberately provincial Galilean, and at that moment gods and nations ceased to be, and humans came into being. This "deliberately provincial Galilean" was a light shining in the darkness of the Roman Empire. It is a light that two-thousand years of history has been unable to extinguish. The love of God as modeled in the life of Jesus is still at work in the world for those who have embraced it. This love gives us hope for living through the darkness of our own time.

Do you agree with Phillip Gulley's definition of love?

How has this definition found expression in your life?

Part V.

AFFIRMATIONS

24.

The Conjunct Life

The holy conjunction ... AND

IN FEBRUARY 1973, I dined with Elton Trueblood for the first time. Trueblood is the author of thirty-eight books and was a professor of religion and philosophy at Harvard, Stanford, and Earlham College. His family had been associated with the Quaker movement for as long as the Newbys. He was considered the dean of American religious writers. I will never forget the impression he made on me, a twenty-three-year-old minister in Central City, Nebraska, nor the topic of our conversation. "James," he said, "What is your sermon topic for next First Day?" This was Monday evening. I had no idea what I was going to speak on next First Day. I had said everything I knew in my ten-minute sermon the past week! "I don't know," I responded. He continued, "I want you to speak on the *holy conjunction, AND*. He then talked about the importance of balance and conjunction in the life of the spirit, a life of *both/and*, rather than *either/or*. To clarify, Elton opened his Bible, which he always carried with him, and turned to that famous question directed to Jesus by the lawyer: "Teacher, which is the greatest commandment in the law?" Jesus responded, "You shall love the Lord your God with all of your heart, *and* with all of your soul, *and* with all of your mind, *and* you shall love your neighbor as yourself." (Matthew 22:37-39) In forty-five minutes over dinner, Elton Trueblood initiated in me a course of thought that continues to this day. In each phase of my spiritual quest, the idea of the holy conjunction has been important. To live a life of conjunction is the key to the spiritual wholeness I seek.

My family can trace its Quaker roots back to northern England in the mid-1600's. The sole deviation to this tradition is my great, great, great grandfather who was "disowned" by his Quaker Meeting for marrying, of all things, a Methodist! No one in my family knew about his disownment until I found a neatly folded piece of paper in my grandfather's Bible. I carefully unfolded it and read these words: "Richard Ricks, having accomplished his marriage contrary to our discipline and having been treated with on the occasion and not manifesting a disposition to condemn his deviation, we therefore disown him from being a member of our Religious Society." The disownment certificate was signed by the Clerk of Short Creek Monthly Meeting in Ohio, on the 18th of the 2nd Month, 1840. (I have often wondered how in 1840 my meeting would have dealt with me for marrying a Hispanic woman from a Roman Catholic and Southern Baptist background!) Fortunately, Quakers have long since abandoned the practice of "disownment."

So, I am a Quaker by *tradition*. As I grew in my personal faith journey, I began to relate more and more to the Quaker passion for social reform and majored in sociology in college. The Quaker testimonies of peace, simplicity, equality, community, integrity and stewardship of the Earth, led me to action. My faith became an anchor for my actions against all forms of injustice, but especially the Vietnam War, and issues surrounding Civil Rights. I was never arrested for my activism, but my fiancé, Elizabeth, and I, came close one time when we were handing out "Boycott Grapes" fliers at a local IGA store in Wichita, Kansas. As noted earlier, Elizabeth and her family were migrant farm workers and while in California had worked closely with Cesar Chavez, the head of the United Farm Workers Union. Chavez was the leader of the "Boycott Grapes" movement, which was formed to protest the pay and working conditions of migrant farm workers. When the manager of the IGA store threatened to call the police, we left peacefully.

My activity on behalf of social reform continues to this day. However, there was another element to my faith journey which was ready to emerge when I met Elton Trueblood. At the time I was in the same condition as Walt Whitman, who said, "I was simmering, simmering, simmering. It was Emerson who brought me to a boil." Elton Trueblood brought me to a boil. He was the impetus that moved me from a merely *tradition-centered* and *activist-centered* faith, to a journey that was centered in the *intellect*. Loving God with my *mind* captivated me, and led me to devour books on philosophy, theology and Biblical studies. When I entered the Earlham School of Religion, my pattern was to take my classes in the morning, and then walk to Teague Library, Elton Trueblood's study on the Earlham campus, and sit with him for the afternoon. We talked about all areas of theology and the Bible, and I studied at the table he provided for his students. I loved those times of learning.

And then my Father died, and my Mother died, and our only child left for college in Michigan, and Elizabeth and I went through a divorce. The intellectual side of my faith was not very helpful in these times when I was experiencing such pain and loss. I felt out of control, and I sought help from those who knew about pain and who shared their lives from a place of authenticity. I was forced to examine my life from the perspective of the *heart*.

Life can be divided into compartments. The dissected life is the opposite of the wholeness I seek. We can be one person at work and another person at home. We can be *tradition-centered only*, or *activist-centered only*, or *intellect-centered only*, or *heart-centered only*. The *conjunct life*, however, is a life lived out in authenticity, and encompasses *all* these elements. A life of *both/and*, not *either/or*, is, I believe, the life of integrated, authentic wholeness that God wants me to live.

Do you seek to live a life of conjunction,
in integrated authentic wholeness?
How has your faith formed who you are?

25.

A Model of Spirituality in A Time of Tribalism

My heart was tender and often contrite,
and a universal love to my fellow
creatures increased in me . . .

THAT WE ARE LIVING in a divisive time is not "breaking news." One *New York Times* reporter called this a time of tribalism, Rich vs. Poor, South vs. North, White vs. Black and Brown, Well Educated vs. Poorly Educated, etc. However defined, it is uncomfortable, and tearing at the fragile fabric that holds us together as a society. We live in an anxiety filled world, and those of us in America live with a president who is one of the great anxiety creators of all time.

I have been thinking lately about the de-sensitizing of American society, and the consequent callous disregard for the feelings and welfare of one another. In her writing, *Of the Empire*, the late Mary Oliver said: "We will be known as a culture that feared death and adored power, that tried to vanquish insecurity for the few and cared little for the many. We will be known as a culture that taught and rewarded the amassing of things, that spoke little if at all about the quality of life for people . . . other people, for dogs, for rivers. All the world, in our eyes, they will say was a commodity. And they will say this structure was held together politically, which it was, and they will say also that our politics was no more than an apparatus to accommodate the feelings of the heart, and that the heart, in those days, was small and hard, and full of meanness."

These are not easy words to read, for we are a part of that time Mary Oliver describes. It is a time when migrant children die in the custody of our government. A Facebook post asked, "If your first response to this news is 'were they illegal?' then we don't have a difference in politics, we have a difference in morals." Bombs and missiles made in America are killing innocent people in Yemen. Racial and political division as well as cultural division, highlight our differences and belittle what we have in common. The gap between the very wealthy and the very poor grows greater. Health insurance companies determine who lives and dies. It is morally reprehensible that people living in the wealthiest country in the world are dying because they can't afford to live.

This hardening of the heart has been going on a long time, although it seems to have been magnified recently. What can Quakers offer as an antidote to such de-sensitizing and de-humanizing experiences? Is there a model of spirituality, someone to whom we can turn who offers a way of life counter to what we all have been experiencing?

I believe there is. One of my spiritual heroes is John Woolman, an eighteenth century Quaker who models a spirituality that was never more needed than now. What is it that makes John Woolman such a moving spiritual figure? Why is it that what he wrote over two-hundred years ago can touch and challenge our hearts today? I would suggest that the reason he is such an important spiritual figure is because Woolman did not just talk about spiritual transformation, he *lived* spiritual transformation throughout his too brief life. Toward the beginning of his famous *Journal*, he writes about his transformation in this way: "While I silently ponder on that change wrought in me, I find no language equal to convey to another any clear idea of it. I looked upon the works of God in this visible creation, and an awfulness covered me. My heart was tender and often contrite, and a universal love to my fellow creatures increased in me."

Woolman succinctly captures the meaning of spiritual transformation. Transformation is expressed in the *tenderizing of one's heart* and increases in *universal love to one's fellow creatures.* What does having one's heart grow tender mean? What are the marks of such a process? How do I begin to experience, and how can our society experience, that sense of awe that finds expression in a tender and contrite heart?

As I have expressed earlier, a profound *sense of spiritual humility* is the first mark of a tender heart. Those persons with tender hearts do not boast or intimidate. They are not braggarts or bullies. The tender hearted are not self-righteous or judgmental. They do not insist on their own way, espousing certitudes that love and reflective thought have not tested. Humility has been part of the lives of all who seek to grow in Spirit and is an important signpost given us by those who have traveled the path of spiritual growth. John Woolman possessed a humility born of a tender heart.

Another mark of a heart growing in love toward God and one another, and which is beautifully illustrated in the life of John Woolman, is a *sense of connection with human suffering.* Within the Christian tradition, a tender heart is a heart that is broken by what breaks the heart of Jesus.

John Woolman felt this connection with suffering in a profound way. In his *Journal* he records a dream in which he saw a mass of matter to the South and the East. As he reflected upon this dream, he became aware that this mass was human beings in great misery. The misery was so great that Woolman could hear their crying and their wails of pain. As he struggled to interpret this dream, Woolman was suddenly enlightened with the insight that he was "mixed with" these people who were suffering, and that he could no longer consider himself distinct or separate. Their suffering was his suffering. Their cries of pain were his cries of pain. They were connected. This connection became a life-long ministry as Woolman spoke out against slavery, particularly among members of the Society of Friends. Philosopher and professor, Alfred North Whitehead said that Woolman stood at that pivotal point in history when we began to envision a civilization without slavery. It is said that Woolman's protests against slavery were so effective among Quakers, that sixty-years before the shot at Fort Sumter that began the Civil War, no Quaker was known to have owned a slave. A sense of connection with human suffering is a characteristic of a tender heart.

Woolman's tender heart was also demonstrated in his *caring and sensitivity toward the entire created order*. A love of all of God's creation is a component of a tender heart. Woolman's heart would break if he were to see pictures of "big game" hunters posing by the corpses of lions, tigers and elephants they had shot. He had a sensitivity shown in his concern for the way that animals were treated by humans, particularly the way horses were treated by carriage drivers. Toward the end of his life when he traveled to England, Woolman refused to ride in carriages because the drivers ran their horses to death to meet too-tight schedules. Instead, Woolman walked everywhere. A tender heart cares for the entire created order.

On a personal note, there is a passage in Woolman's *Journal* where he writes about my sixth- great grandfather, who brought a concern to Woolman while my relative was taking him from one speaking engagement to another in North Carolina. Samuel Newby's conscience bothered him about paying taxes, because so much of this money went to pay for war. He told Woolman that he was thinking about not paying that portion of those taxes, and asked Woolman for his advice. Woolman replied that he had a like concern, and that his conscience was also bothered. Whether or not my sixth great-grandfather acted on his concern, I do not know.

More than any other person in the history of the Society of Friends, John Woolman lived the Quaker testimonies. He lived a life of simplicity and worked for peace in our diverse world. He lived a life of integrity, and he loved his community and meeting at Mt. Holly, New Jersey. Woolman worked tirelessly on issues of equality, and he felt a sense of stewardship for all of God's creation.

If there was ever a need for the spirituality that John Woolman lived, it is *now*.

In his pamphlet, *A Plea for The Poor*, Woolman wrote from his tender heart and his increasing love for all: "Our gracious Creator cares and provides for all his Creatures. His tender mercies are over all his works; and so far as his love influences our minds, so far as we become interested in his workmanship, and feel a desire to take hold of every opportunity to lessen the distresses of the afflicted and increase the happiness of the Creation. Here we have a prospect of one common interest, from which our own is inseparable, that *to turn all of the treasures that we possess into the channel of Universal Love, becomes the business of our lives.*"

*As you grow spiritually, how is your heart
becoming more tender?*

*How are you lessening the distresses of the afflicted in our
society, and increasing the happiness of the Creation?*

26.

The Peacemakers

We utterly deny all outward wars and
strife and fightings with outward weapons,
for any end or under any pretense whatsoever.

IN 1661, THE EARLY Quakers sent a Declaration to King
Charles II. It read, in part, "We utterly deny all outward wars and
strife and fightings with outward weapons, for any end or under
any pretense whatsoever. And this is our testimony to the whole
world. The Spirit of Christ, by which we are guided, is not change-
able, so as once to command us from a thing as evil and again
to move unto it; and we do certainly know, and so testify to the
world, that the Spirit of Christ, which leads us into all Truth, will
never move us to fight and war against any person with outward
weapons, neither for the kingdom of Christ, nor for the kingdoms
of this world."

A testimony on peace is one of main tenets of the people
called Quakers. From the beginning Quakers have sought to be
peacemakers and to live in the Light and Love that takes away the
occasion for war. Many would call this impractical. Conversely, I
suggest that war and violence are not "practical," and in the words
of William Penn, whom Thomas Jefferson called "the greatest

lawgiver the world has ever produced," "It is time to see what *love can do.*"

We live in a time of terror and fear. One way or another, violence seems a part of everyday life. America has known war since its inception, with little respite between conflicts. Today, the United States prosecutes never-ending wars in Afghanistan, Iraq, Syria, and Yemen. At home, a gun culture underlies far too many injuries and killings. Being a peacemaker in such a time as this is not easy.

One person whom most people revere as an example of a life lived with God, is Mother Teresa. As the reader may have noted, I am a great admirer of her life and writings. I think Mother Teresa was a Quaker in a former life. In her *Reflections on Working Toward Peace*, Mother Teresa shares these important words: "The fruit of silence is prayer, the fruit of prayer is faith; the fruit of love is service; the fruit of service is peace. Let us not use bombs and guns to overcome the world. Let us use love and compassion. Let us radiate the peace of God and light, His Light and extinguish in the world and in the hearts of all people all hatred and love for power. Today if we have no peace, it is because we have forgotten that we belong to each other. That man, that woman, that child is my brother or sister. If everyone could see the image of God in his or her neighbor, do you think we would still need tanks and generals?

"Peace and war begin at home. If we truly want peace in the world, let us begin by loving one another in our own families. If we want to spread joy, we need for every family to have joy." Perhaps Mother Teresa is too simple, or as the Quakers have been called, impractical. I am convinced, however, that the path to peace begins with such small, simple steps.

Thomas Cahill, the author of *How the Irish Saved Civilization*, wrote, "What will be lost and what saved of our civilization probably lies beyond our powers to decide. The future may be germinating today not in a boardroom in London or an office in Washington, or a bank in Tokyo, but in some antic outpost, a kindly British orphanage in the grim foothills of Peru, a house for the dying in a back street of Calcutta, a mission to Somalia by Irish social workers who remember their own great hunger, in some unheralded corner where a great hearted human being is committed to loving outcasts in an extraordinary way. The twenty-first century will be spiritual, or it will not be. If our civilization is to be saved, it will be saved by saints."

It is tempting to tell ourselves that we cannot make a difference regarding peace among nations or even peace on the streets where we live. Perhaps. But this rationalization should not prevent people from trying, from trying to become a people who love outcasts in an extraordinary way. We can all work for justice.

And we can pray and hold others in the Light. In his, *The Rise and Progress of the People Called Quakers*, an introduction to the *Journal of George Fox*, the founder of the people called Quakers, William Penn wrote, "But above all he excelled in prayer. The inwardness and weight of his spirit, the reverence and solemnity of his address, and behavior, and the fewness and fullness of his words, have often struck even strangers with admiration, as they used to reach others with consolation. The most awful, living, reverent frame I ever felt or beheld, I must say, was his in prayer."

Along with spiritual giants through the centuries, we too can recognize *prayer* as the first step toward peace. We can become a people who pray and hold our leaders in the Light, so that all those with the power to make decisions will find the way to peace.

The truth is we already know the way. We just need the will to get there. The way to peace is through justice for the poor, the hungry, and thirsty, whether that hunger be physical, spiritual, or political. The way to peace is through common sense gun legislation that keeps firearms out of the hands of persons filled with hate and grievance. The way to peace is to focus on peaceful solutions to conflict, rather than too quickly resorting to violence. The way to peace is through a spiritual transformation, so that we finally recognize, in the radical way that John Donne, the seventeenth century dean of St. Paul's Cathedral in London, came to recognize,

No person is an island, and that as a part of the human family we belong to one another. And we can hold one another in the Light. "Blessed are the peacemakers," said Jesus, "for they will be called children of God." (Matthew 5:9)

What do you believe are the obstacles to peace?

In what ways can you work for peace, in your families, your communities, and in the world?

27.

A Theology of Experience, Relationship, Justice and Journey

You cannot step into the same rivers;
for fresh waters are ever flowing in upon you.

EVER SINCE I WAS a boy, I have asked myself, "What do I believe?" and "Why do I believe it?" Belief is important. What we believe will be the impetus to how we act out our faith. In brief, what we believe is *ortho-doxy*, or "right thinking or belief," will issue in *ortho-practice*, or "right living and practice."

I recognize the wide diversity of belief within the body of Christian believers, as well as the diversity of belief within and between all faith traditions. Each person must make his or her own way through the maze of questions, absurdities, and incoherent patterns of life, validating a belief system by personal experience. Only then does one's faith become a *living faith*. The following are the primary elements in my own spiritual journey, which is still *in process*.

I often refer to myself as an *experiential, relational, justice focused*, and *journey* theologian. Each term helps me to define the experience of God in my life. *Experience is the touchstone of all that I believe* and is the *first* piece in the construction of my theology.

This is what keeps my faith vibrant and alive and forms the basis for my actions in the world. "Immediate experience" was the impetus for the Quaker mission of George Fox, and over the years Quakers have produced thousands of writings that share their personal spiritual experiences. We are a people of transformation and experience. In his classic, *The Varieties of Religious Experience*, Harvard psychologist, William James, declared: "If you ask for a concrete example (of religious experience), there can be no better one than is furnished by the person of George Fox. The Quaker religion which he founded is something which it is impossible to over praise. In a day of shams, it was a religion of veracity, rooted in spiritual inwardness."

While I was minister of faith and learning at the Wayzata Community Church in Minnesota, I invited Elaine Pagels of Princeton University to come and share about her work on the Gnostic gospels. In her engaging style, she kept a group of over six-hundred captivated describing her research on the Nag Hammadi Texts, which were discovered in Upper Egypt by an Arab peasant in December 1945. These writings have greatly helped the Christian world understand how our faith was formed, what has become "Orthodox Christian Belief," and what was discarded as heresy. An important part of Gnostic belief was centered on personal experience, which Pagels argues was rejected too soon. Necessary as it seemed to many in the early church to expel heretics, or those who believed that personal spiritual experience was a threat to "correct" thought that they defended, expulsion impoverished both the church and those expelled. While guarding against the eccentricities of subjectivism, religious experience has been the major fuel of spirituality, and is the touchstone of my faith.

To prevent eccentricity, I acknowledge dependence on others to help me interpret my experiences. All experiences should be tested. Quakers have what we call, "clearness committees" to examine experiences within community. I acknowledge that I need others to help me discern and evaluate my spiritual experiences.

A second part of my personal theology is *relationship*. I come to know God in my relationships with others. I believe that there is that of God in everyone. Responding to the question, "What is the greatest commandment?" Jesus included love of neighbor along with love of God. God is certainly beyond us, but God is also within us. My understanding of God is broadened and deepened as I interact with others, whether feeding the hungry, visiting those in prison, encouraging the discouraged, or sitting with another discussing our lives over a beer or a cup of coffee.

My understanding of relational theology also extends beyond the human world to the world of nature. As I write, it is a very dark and cold March day in Cincinnati, Ohio. A few flakes of snow are falling, and there is a slight breeze. In the distance two deer forage for food and periodically look up at passing cars. Trying not to dwell on the upcoming spring, I seek, instead, to experience the here and now and my oneness with this hour and this day. As a relational theologian I know that my interactions in the natural world are important to my understanding of how God interacts with me. In the miracle of the natural world and the season of winter, I can feel the presence of God.

A third part of my developing theology is *justice focused*. I do not consider myself a being apart from the rest of humanity. If anyone experiences injustice, then I am experiencing injustice. Whenever and wherever people are not treated fairly, or are used and abused to enrich others, I feel I must help them find justice. The God that I worship is a God of justice, and I am grateful for my Quaker faith which has led in fighting injustice since its beginning.

The pursuit of justice is a part of who my family has been and who I have become. Our family took the Quaker testimony on equality seriously. My mother and father instilled within me and my siblings the story of the decades-long pursuit of justice by African Americans. My Friends Meeting, my mother's work with Church Women United, and my father's work as the chair of the Mayor's Commission on Human Relations in both Minneapolis, Minnesota and Muncie, Indiana, introduced me at a very young age to the struggle for racial equality in America. My wife, Elizabeth, and I have been involved with justice concerns surrounding America's treatment of migrant farmworkers and Hispanic workers in general. I know that this country's history is not a saga of equal justice for all, as so many would like to believe and hope. The way in which the belief in Manifest Destiny led to the wholesale killing of Native Americans, and the lasting effects of slavery, the Original Sin of the United States continue to haunt us. The Chinese Exclusion Act of 1882, and the turning away of the German ship, St. Louis, in 1939, carrying 937 Jewish refugees from Nazi Germany, have stained the words on the Statue of Liberty, "Give me your tired, your poor, your huddled masses yearning to breathe free." And now brown people at our southern border, in what can only be described as blatant racism, are being told by our president that they are not welcome here, and that our nation "is full." The God of justice and love that I worship weeps at these mean-spirited actions.

A final part of my theology can be described in the word, *journey*, which can be understood as a synonym for *process*. Professor and writer, Alfred North Whitehead, is the best-known process thinker, but the roots of process can be traced to Heraclitus, who said, "You cannot step into the same rivers; for fresh waters are ever flowing in upon you." At the core, journey theology is the belief that everything in the world is in a state of flux, and that everything is in process toward becoming something. George Malley, a character played by John Travolta in the movie, *Phenomenon*, opined "Everything is on its way somewhere." We are all on a journey, and God is interacting with us in each moment of this journey.

A few years ago, I designed an adult education program called, "Nurturing Experience Theologically," or "NET Groups." Two questions at the center of the program, and which I encouraged participants to ask of every experience were, "How is God working here?" and "What spiritual lesson or lessons am I to learn?" As Whitehead stated, "God is a richly related being whose innermost nature is in his ceaseless participation and sharing."

I will always be in the process of developing a framework for what I believe and why I believe it. Within my soul, such a chapter as this is always being written, changed, added to, and so forth. The following *Credo* summarizes my thoughts and feelings. For now, this is where I am on my journey.

What are the basic parts of your personal theology?

Have you ever attempted to write a personal credo?

Epilogue

A Personal Credo: God of the Double Search

This is the God of the double search, who I seek in my spiritual quest, and who is also seeking me.

AUTHOR'S NOTE: THIS *PERSONAL* credo emerged at a time when many of the old pedestals on which my faith rested were beginning to crumble. The reader may disagree with what I share. I recognize that we are all on differing spiritual paths. I do, however, hope that the reader can acknowledge the sincere and heartfelt feelings from which these words have come.

God of the Double Search

I no longer believe in God who sits high above the clouds
and dispenses wrath at will, and for whom
excuses must be made
when children are killed and hurricanes strike,
and AIDS takes the life of a friend.

I do, however, believe in a God of love and incarnation,
A God who is real, and who suffers with me, and
laughs with me, and who walks with me in the darkest
times of doubt but, nonetheless, lets me doubt.

I believe in a God who is still loving and creating,
a God who is still forgiving and blessing,
who is still evolving in process with me,
who shares my joys and my sorrows.

I believe in a God of passion and pain,
a God whom I can explore in prayer and dance with in paradox.
A God who is on journey with me, and in whom
resides the soul of a child, opening to me passageways
into the eternal.
This is a God in whom I can believe,
who can be experienced in the beauty of nature and
is reflected in the eyes of a struggling humanity.
This is the God of the double search, the God I seek in my spiritual quest,
and who is also seeking me.

Bibliography

Augustine, Saint. *The Confessions of St. Augustine*. New York: Modern Library, 1949.

Barclay, Robert. *The Apology*. Philadelphia, 1908.

Bianco, Williams Margery. *The Velveteen Rabbit*. Garden City, New York: Doubleday, 1982.

Bill, J. Brent. *Holy Silence*. Brewster, Massachusetts: Paraclete, 2005.

Borg, Marcus. *Meeting Jesus Again for the First Time*. San Francisco: Harper Collins, 1994.

Boulding, Kenneth. *There Is a Spirit: The Nayler Sonnets*. New York: Fellowship, 1945.

Braithwaite, William. *The Beginnings of Quakerism, Vol. I.* New York: Macmillan, 1912.

Buechener, Frederick. *The Sacred Journey*. New York: Harper Collins, 1982.

Cahill, Thomas. *How the Irish Saved Civilization*. New York: Nan A. Talese, 1995.

Camus, Albert. *The Plague*. (Translated by Stuart Gilbert) London: Penguin, 1960.

Delbanco, Andrew. PBS Series, *America Responds*. An Interview with Bill Moyers, September 12, 2001.

Delio, Ilia. *Compassion: Living in the Spirit of Saint Francis*. Cincinnati: Franciscan Media and Servant Books, 2011.

Dickens, Charles. *A Christmas Carol*. London: Chapman and Hall, 1843.

Fournier, Ron and Sophie Quinton. "In Nothing We Trust." Washington, DC. *The Atlantic* magazine, April 19, 2012.

Fox, George. *The Journal of George Fox*. Edited by John Nickalls. Philadelphia Yearly Meeting, 1997.

Fulghum, Robert. *All I Really Need to Know I Learned in Kindergarten*. New York: Villard Books, 1988.

Gibran, Kahil. *The Prophet*. New York: Alfred A. Knopf, 1923.

Gulley, Philip. *Living the Quaker Way*. New York: Convergent Books, 2013.

———. *Unlearning God*. New York: Convergent Books, 2018.

Hoff, Ben. *The Tao of Pooh*. New York: E.P. Dutton, 1982.

James, William. *The Varieties of Religious Experience*. New York: Penguin, 1982.

Kavanaugh, James. *Will You Be My Friend?* San Francisco: Harper and Row, 1984.

Kazantzakis, Nikos. *Zorba the Greek*. New York: Simon and Schuster, 1953.

Keen, Sam. *Fire in the Belly*. New York: Bantam, 1992.

———. "What You Ask is Who You Are." Kahului, Hawaii: *Spirituality and Health* magazine, May 1, 2000.

Kelly, Thomas. *A Testament of Devotion*. New York: Harper and Brothers, 1941.

Kerr, Hugh T. and Mulder, John M. *Conversions*. Grand Rapids: Wm. B. Eerdmans, 1983.

Lynd, Robert and Helen Merrell. *Middletown: A Study in Modern American Culture*. New York: Harcourt Brace and Company, 1929.

Milne, A.A. *Winnie-The-Pooh*. London: Methuen, 1926.

Mother Teresa. *Reflections on Working Toward Peace*. Santa Clara University, Santa Clara, California: Architects of Peace.

Nayler, James. *See* Boulding, Kenneth.

Newby, James R. *Sacred Chaos: One Man's Journey Through Pain and Loss*, New York: Continuum, 1998.

———. *Shining Out and Shining In*. Bloomington, Indiana: AuthorHouse, 2013.

Oliver, Mary. "Of the Empire." *Dream Work*. New York: Grove, 2010.

Pagels, Elaine. *Why Religion?* New York: Harper Collins, 2018.

Pasternak, Boris. *Doctor Zhivago*. Italy: Pantheon, 1957.

Patton, Kimberly. "When the Wounded Emerge as Healers." Cambridge, Massachusetts: *Harvard Divinity Bulletin*, Winter, 2006.

Penn, William. *The Rise and Progress of the People Called Quakers*. Richmond, Indiana: Friends United Press, 1977.

Quindlen, Anna. "Life of the Closed Mind." New York: *Newsweek* magazine, May 29, 2005.

White, E.B. *Charlotte's Web*. New York: Harper and Brothers, 1952.

Whitehead, Alfred North. *Adventures of Ideas*. New York: The Free Press, 1967.

Whittier, John Greenleaf. *Whittier's Poems*. Chicago: Donohue, 1900.

Will, George. "The Oddness of Everything." New York: *Newsweek* magazine, May 22, 2005.

Woolman, John. *The Journal and Major Essays of John Woolman*. Edited by Amelia Mott Gummere. New York: Macmillan, 1922.